SpringerBriefs in Computer Science

For further volumes:
http://www.springer.com/series/10028

Anna Sidorova · Nicholas Evangelopoulos
Russell Torres · Vess Johnson

A Survey of Core Research in Information Systems

Springer

Anna Sidorova
Nicholas Evangelopoulos
Russell Torres
Vess Johnson
University of North Texas
Denton, TX
USA

ISSN 2191-5768 ISSN 2191-5776 (electronic)
ISBN 978-1-4614-7157-8 ISBN 978-1-4614-7158-5 (eBook)
DOI 10.1007/978-1-4614-7158-5
Springer New York Heidelberg Dordrecht London

Library of Congress Control Number: 2013934098

Printed on acid-free paper

Springer is part of Springer Science+Business Media (www.springer.com)

Preface

For the IS discipline to balance focus and diversity, how can it best deal with the proliferation of research topics and terminologies? How can we as IS researchers keep the discipline from degenerating into a Babel tower of research? In his discussion on the role of scientific paradigms, Kuhn places particular emphasis on textbooks as tools of academic communication. He argues that education in paradigmatic fields is characterized by the dominance of textbooks which summarize and often streamline the past developments in the field. Textbooks help scientists within the field to develop a common vocabulary, which enhances the efficiency of scientific communication. In Kuhn's words, "Textbooks themselves aim to communicate the vocabulary and syntax of a contemporary scientific language" (Kuhn 1996, p. 136).

Unfortunately, little of the academic education of future IS scholars is textbook based. While many high quality textbooks exist at the undergraduate and Master's levels, these textbooks are only partially useful for building background knowledge for future IS scholars. At these levels, IS education focuses on providing students with ready-to-apply skills (often technical in nature). Consequently, most of the existing textbooks aim at presenting existing practical methods and approaches for managing IT, rather than building the theoretical background required by future IS researchers. As a result, much of doctoral education is based on the reading of original research publications in research journals. While highly valuable from the perspective of exposing students to the best exemplars of IS scholarship, this is hardly the most efficient way for providing a broad overview of IS scholarship, or for building a holistic understanding of the IS research.

With this publication, we hope to make the first step in establishing a textbook tradition in doctoral IS education. In this book we provide a high level overview of the key research topics in IS. Emerging and current IS scholars can use it as a tool for quickly acquainting themselves with the different topics of IS research. In each of the areas, we simply summarize the directions of research efforts, rather than providing interpretations or explanations of such efforts. For each topic we direct the readers to some of the important related research publications.

The chapters included in this book are organized as follows. In Chap. 1 we provide an introduction to the IS discipline and certain debates that played an instrumental role in its development. Chapter 2 presents the intellectual structure of the body of IS research in terms of the five main research areas. Chapter 2 also discusses topics that concern IS discipline in general, including IS discipline debates, theories and methods in IS, and instrument development in IS research. Chapters 3 through 7 provide an overview of research topics in the key IS research areas, including *IT artifact and IS development*, *IT and organizations*, *IT and individuals*, *IT and markets*, and *IT for teamwork and collaboration*. Finally, Chap. 8 summarizes the structure of academic research in IS and offers concluding remarks. The details of a bibliometric study used to identify the key research topics in IS presented in this book are provided in the Appendix.

Denton, TX, December 2012

Anna Sidorova
Nicholas Evangelopoulos
Russell Torres
Vess Johnson

Contents

Chapter 1
Introduction

The information revolution powered by information technology is changing the way in which knowledge work is performed and organizations are managed. Information and communication technology (ICT) has permeated all areas of business, from supply chain management to intra-office communication. Personal activities from shopping to driving have been influenced by information technology. Technological advances are accompanied by dramatic changes in society. The fusion of computing and communication devices and their increased portability lead to the blurring of lines between computer use and non-use, between work-related and recreational use of computers and, ultimately, between work and leisure. The increasingly sophisticated analytical algorithms, coupled with ever powerful computers threaten to sideline human decision makers in favor of algorithm-based decisions (Vance 2012). The interaction between information technology, business, and society at large is multifaceted and multidirectional. Information systems research aims to study such interaction, and to help harness the power of ICT in order to improve business and the life of individuals.

1.1 The Information Systems Discipline

The Information Systems (IS) discipline sprung up in the 1970s in response to the need to understand the role and the impact of information technology in the organizational context. It was originally comprised of academics from a variety of backgrounds, from computer science, to economics, to management. The formal establishment of the IS discipline can be traced to the publication of the inaugural issue of Management Information Systems Quarterly in March 1977. Shortly after that, in December 1980, the first meeting of the International Conference on Information Systems (ICIS) took place. Information Systems has since been established as one of the main business disciplines, along with management, marketing, accounting, finance, and management science. The Association for Information Systems, a professional association that brings together IS academics

A. Sidorova et al., *A Survey of Core Research in Information Systems*,
SpringerBriefs in Computer Science, DOI: 10.1007/978-1-4614-7158-5_1,

and research-oriented practitioners, was founded in the mid-1990s, and by the early 2010s it boasted having members from 90 different countries (AIS Website, 2012, http://start.aisnet.org/?AboutAIS). The IS discipline is represented by a variety of prestigious research journals (see Table 1.1), with MIS Quarterly strongly positioned among the most influential business journals, as measured by the ISI citation index (Dean et al. 2011).

The development of the IS discipline has been accompanied by several existential debates, usually involving top IS researchers. Such debates aim at establishing directions for the future course of the discipline. The more notable debates deal with the issues of IS discipline identity and diversity and the balance between rigor and relevance in IS research. The IS identity and diversity debates are of particular relevance to the purpose of this book, and are discussed in the next Sect. 1.2.[1]

1.2 The Identity Debate

The identity debate is concerned with establishing the cognitive legitimacy of the IS discipline vis-à-vis its more established counterparts, many of which have served as reference disciplines for IS research. The central question of the debate is: What are the appropriate phenomena of study for the IS discipline, and should IS research be restricted to those areas? The origins of the debate can be traced back to a paper presented at the inaugural ICIS conference by Peter Keen. Keen suggests that, in order to establish the IS discipline as a "classical area", IS academics should identify reference disciplines, clearly define the dependent variable and figure out how to build a cumulative tradition (Keen 1980). Consequently, much of the identity discourse has focused on what is, and what is not, an appropriate variable of interest for IS researchers (looking for the dependent variable), positioning the IS discipline vis-à-vis other academic disciplines (the reference disciplines), and trying to build a cumulative tradition.

The IS success model was proposed in response to Keen's call for defining the dependent variable of interest to IS researchers (Delone and McLean 1992). Drawing on the seminal work of Shannon and Weaver (1949) and Mason (1978), the model frames the dependent variable of the IS discipline in terms of IS success categories, such as system quality, information quality, use, user satisfaction, individual impact, and organizational impact. The IS success model was updated to include service quality as an antecedent of use and user satisfaction. Intention to use was added as a close relative of the system use category, and individual and organizational benefits were merged into the net benefits category (Delone and McLean 2003). The IS success model has had a profound influence on subsequent

[1] Chapter 2 provides review of the literature devoted to the development of the IS discipline, and thus provides a more comprehensive overview of other debates.

Table 1.1 Selected IS Research Journals

Journal Name	Year establ.	Issues per year (2011)	Articles per year (2011)	2004–2007 ISI Impact Factor average (Dean et al. 2011)	2011 ISI 5-year Impact Factor (ISI JCR 2011)
MIS Quarterly (MISQ)	1977	4	50	4.604	7.497
Information Systems Research (ISR)	1990	4	47	2.696	4.131
Journal of MIS (JMIS)	1984	4	40	1.590	2.945
Journal of the AIS (JAIS)	2000	12	28	n/a	2.654
European Journal of Information Systems (EJIS)	1992	6	43	0.917	2.218
Information Systems Journal (ISJ)	1991	6	21	1.090	2.775
Information and Management (I&M)	1977	8	44	1.772	3.796
Decision Support Systems (DSS)	1985	8	148	1.171	2.331
International Journal of E-Commerce (IJEC)	1996	4	20	1.200	2.426
Journal of Database Management (JDM)	1990	4	16	1.690	0.779
Journal of Strategic Information Systems	1991	4	29	0.750	2.000
Journal of Information Technology	1986	4	19	1.309	3.000

Journal name abbreviations indicated in this table are used to refer to the journals in the reference section

IS research, and has been used as an organizing framework for reviewing IS literature (Clark et al. 2007).

The search for the dependent variable has later been restated as the search for the core of the IS discipline. The IT artifact nomological net proposed by Benbasat and Zmud (2003) outlines the core of the IS discipline in terms of factors that influence and that are influenced by the IT artifact. Such factors are grouped into four categories: (1) IT methodological and technological capabilities, (2) IT managerial, methodological and operational practices, (3) IT usage and (4) IT impact. The authors caution that focusing on research questions not directly related to any of the aforementioned factors may lead to the dilution of the boundaries between IS and its reference disciplines, and impede the establishment of the cognitive legitimacy of the IS discipline. While the main premise of the Benbasat and Zmud's opinion piece was widely debated, the IT artifact nomological net remains a highly influential framework for identifying the core of IS research.

1.3 The Focus Versus Diversity Discourse

Related to the efforts to define the phenomena of interests in IS research, a debate over the need to establish a cumulative research tradition has taken place. While the need for a cumulative research tradition was pointed out by Keen (1980), progress in this direction has been relatively slow, with many prominent scholars opposing the idea that IS research needs to be forced into a single paradigm. Framing the cumulative tradition debate, Banville and Landry posed the question "Can the MIS field be disciplined?" as the title of their *Communication of the ACM* article (Banville and Landry 1989). Building on the Whitley's scientific field classification model based on such characteristics as strategic dependence, functional dependence and strategic task uncertainty, the authors classified the MIS field as a fragmented adhocracy, characterized by low degree of strategic and functional dependence and high task uncertainty.

The discourse over the need to establish a cumulative tradition has morphed into the diversity versus focus debate with the Benbasat and Weber's (1996) call for "rethinking diversity in IS research" (p. 389). Initially diversity was pursued in the form of borrowing theories and research approaches from reference disciplines as a path to achieve rigor and gain respect from colleagues in more established academic fields. This has arguably resulted in the excessive theoretical and topical diversity which threatened the cognitive legitimacy of the IS discipline (Benbasat and Weber 1996; Benbasat and Zmud 2003). The calls for a narrower focus in IS research were embraced by some but opposed by others, who argued that the requirement of a strong central core is unnecessary and that the IS research is trans-disciplinary in nature (Galliers 2003; Lyytinen and King 2004). Moreover, the opponents argued that tighter focus may weaken the discipline by stifling academic freedom and turning away potential contributors (Robey 2003).

Many believe that identity anxiety should be put aside and researchers should push forward aggressively and cross boundaries where necessary in order to pursue quality research (King and Lyytinen 2004). In recent years, several empirical assessments of the intellectual structure of the IS research found that strong core and diversity can co-exist in IS research (Sidorova et al. 2008). Furthermore, such co-existence of focus and diversity is natural for an applied discipline, which seeks to balance academic rigor with practical relevance (Taylor et al. 2010). In this book we embrace the view that the IS discipline should seek to balance focus and diversity. We propose that by developing a tradition of summarization of academic IS research, IS scholars can enable sufficient communication across different IS research areas, and thus ensure that the benefits of diversity are fully realized, while its threats are adequately mitigated.

Chapter 2
The Structure of IS Research and IS Discipline Development

Following the results of the bibliometric study presented in the Appendix, we define the structure of IS research in terms of five research areas and 51 research topics. The identified research areas closely mirror those in the Sidorova et al. (2008) study.[1] The research areas include *IT artifact and IS development*, *IT and organizations*, *IT and individuals*, *IT and markets*, *and IT for teamwork and collaboration*. Our ability to replicate the results of the earlier study with an expanded basket of journals and an updated time frame suggests that these areas represent a robust intellectual core of the IS discipline.

At a more detailed level, IS research can described through a number of research topics (51 topics for the purpose of this study). For the complete list of the 51 topics, see Table A2 in the Appendix. The topics are related to one or more research areas. Examples of research topics that lie almost exclusively within one research area (IT artifact and IS development) include *business intelligence and data mining* and *rule based systems*. Similarly, such topics as *IT investments and firm value* and *supply chain management* are primarily organizational in focus, whereas research on *individual IS acceptance and use* almost entirely falls within the *IT and individuals* research area.

The exclusive fit of the research topics with only one research area is an exception, rather than a rule. The majority of the identified topics have a primary and a secondary research area. For example, such topics as *electronic data interchange* and *supply chain management* lie at the intersection of *IT and organizations (primary area),* and *IT and markets* (secondary area). Similarly, such topics as *software development* and *IS security* are primarily organizational in focus; yet both topics also cover *IT artifact and IS development* issues.

Several research topics are almost equally split between two or more research areas. For example, *cultural issues in IS* are addressed almost in equal parts at organizational and individual levels. *On-line consumer behavior* is an almost equal split between *IT and individuals* and *IT and markets*, and knowledge management

[1] This is not surprising as we intentionally sought to methodologically replicate the results of the study by Sidorova et al. (2008), albeit with expanded journal basket and different timeframe.

A. Sidorova et al., *A Survey of Core Research in Information Systems*,
SpringerBriefs in Computer Science, DOI: 10.1007/978-1-4614-7158-5_2,

deals in almost equal manner with issues of *IT artifact and IS development*, *IT and organizations* and *IT for collaboration and teamwork.*

In spite of the loose correspondence between research areas and topics, the five research areas are useful for organizing the review of the literature within individual research topics. Thus, chapters three through seven are devoted to the review of topics that are most closely associated with the corresponding research areas. Reviews of topics that lie at the intersection of two or more research areas are inclusive, and are not limited to the part of the topic associated with the dominant research area. For example, the review of on-line consumer behavior research includes research related to the IT and markets, as well as individual use of IT, even though the review is presented as a part of Chap. 6, IT and Markets.

Three research topics deserve treatment outside of the individual research areas as they pertain to the IS discipline as a whole. These topics include: F31—IS discipline. F1—IS theories, frameworks, and methods; and F13—instrument development and validation. These are reviewed next.

2.1 IS Discipline Development

As discussed in Chap. 1, the development of the IS discipline has been characterized by a plethora of existential debates over such issues as the identity of the IS discipline and the importance of focus versus diversity in IS research. Other discourses focused on the current role and the future of IS as a reference discipline, as well as the importance of rigor versus relevance in IS scholarship. In addition, a number of relatively pragmatic discussions of issues facing IS academics, from journal rankings to tenure and promotion criteria, took place. All related publications are combined under the IS Discipline topic.

The diversity in research topics and identity debates are primarily concerned with defining the boundaries of IS research. The key aspects of these debates are examined in Chap. 1. Yet a discipline is not defined simply by the topics that are researched. It is also defined by the basic assumptions regarding the role of theory and empirical evidence, methodological approaches, key stakeholders, as well as by the institutional structures such as research journals and assessment standards.

Several empirical studies have examined methodological diversity in IS (Orlikowski and Baroudi 1991; Vessey et al. 2002). In contrast with considerable diversity in research topics and reference disciplines, lower level of diversity was identified in relation to research approaches (Orlikowski and Baroudi 1991; Vessey et al. 2002). As a result, calls were made for the IS discipline to move from a predominantly positivist perspective to embrace more interpretive studies (Alavi and Carlson 1992; Chen and Hirschheim 2004). The relationship of the IS discipline with reference disciplines has received significant attention (Wade et al. 2006; Grover et al. 2006), which is not surprising given the high reliance of IS research on reference disciplines, and the high level of diversity in the reference disciplines used in IS research. Results of studies suggest that, while the IS discipline has made a modest impact on other disciplines it has not yet reached the status of a reference discipline (Wade et al. 2006).

The relationship between IS research and practice represents another issue critical to the development of the IS discipline. Established to address an immediate business need to understand and predict the consequences of computerization of the workplace, the IS discipline is by its nature an applied discipline. Yet, in its quest to gain legitimacy and position itself among the more established academic disciplines, IS academics placed significant emphasis on academic rigor, often at the expense of producing research relevant to IS practitioners.

Calls for increasing the relevance of IS research were made from late 1990s to early 2010s (Benbasat and Zmud 1999; Lytinen 1999, Straub and Ang 2008), but the IS academics continue to disagree on the means of achieving an acceptable balance between rigor and relevance. Several approaches to increasing the relevance of IS research have been proposed, ranging from the radical approaches of emulating medical and legal professions (Davenport and Markus 1999), to the more moderate approaches of institutionalizing applicability checks (Roseman and Vessey 2008), marshaling the practical experience of the doctoral students (Klein and Rowe 2008), adjusting the writing style of research publications, and utilizing a variety of ways to disseminate IS research (Straub and Ang 2008). Unfortunately, the rigor-relevance balance remains an elusive goal for IS academics (Gill and Bhattacherjee 2009); therefore, the rigor versus relevance debate is likely to continue into the future.

In addition to the recurring discourses outlined above, a significant share of IS-discipline-related publications is focused on issues related to the everyday operation of the discipline. A number of studies are concerned with ranking and characterizing IS journals. Examples include studies of publications and citations data in order to rank journals (Gallivan and Benbunan-Fich 2007), assessments of journal quality and suitability for IS research (Chua et al. 2003; Lewis et al. 2007), and examinations of relative journal influence using social network analysis (Polites and Watson 2009). A number of publications focus on research productivity of individual researchers and their institutions, as well as tenure and promotion standards (Dean et al. 2011; Dennis et al. 2006; Gallivan and Benbunan-Fich 2007).

A peak in research in the IS discipline occurred in the mid-2000s (corresponding to the renewed identity debate). However, in 2009–2011 publications levels returned to the levels common in 1999–2001 period. As many of the debates concern the perennial issues of the IS discipline development, they are likely to continue attracting attention as the discipline moves forward (Fig. 2.1).

2.2 IS Theory and Methods

IS Theories, Frameworks and Methods: The diverse and multidisciplinary nature of the IS discipline is evident from the variety of theoretical perspectives and methodological approaches that co-exist in IS research. Bridging the technical

Fig. 2.1 Trends for articles on the IS discipline

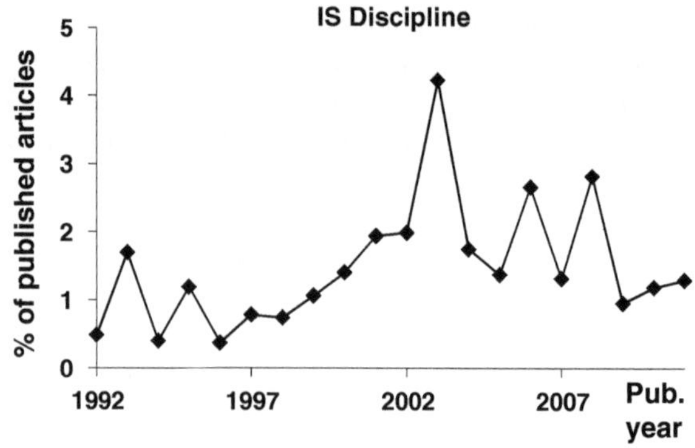

and social domains, the IS discipline draws on the social science as well as engineering research traditions. The social science tradition is represented by the economics-based and behavioral research, whereas the engineering tradition is epitomized by the design science approach in IS research.

The behavioral research tradition is represented by theories that can be broadly characterized along the following dimensions: causal agency, logical structure and level of analysis (Markus and Robey 1989). Causal agency refers to the assumption espoused by the theory regarding the causal agent, which is used to categorize theories into technological imperative, organizational imperative and emergent perspectives. The technological imperative perspective assumes the deterministic role of IT. The IS success model (DeLone and McLean 1992), as well as much of DSS, GSS and website design research is characterized by the technological imperative. The organizational imperative suggests that organizational change occurs as a result of the efforts of IS designers and developers, as well as free-will actions of IT users. The perspective is evident in the individual and organizational IT adoption and use research (Lamb and King 2003), as well as IS management literature. The emergent perspective suggests that technology and human actors interact, and such interaction results in the often un-intended use and consequences of IT. The structuration theory (Orlikowski 1992; Orlikowski and Robey 1991), and the adaptive structuration theory are among the better known examples of the emergent perspective in IS research.

The logical structure of theory refers to the relationship between dependent and independent variables (Markus and Robey 1989). Theories can be classified into variance and process theories. In variance theories, a change in the independent variable is assumed to be a necessary and sufficient condition for the change in the dependent variable. Technology acceptance theories (Davis et al. 1989, etc.), the IS success model (DeLone and McLean 1992), as well as much of the IS research conducted using positivist research methods is variance-theory based. In process theories, changes in independent variables are assumed to be a necessary, but not sufficient condition for the change in the dependent variable. IS theories are formulated at different levels on analysis, including system, individual, group, and organizational levels, with some theories seeking to explain how changes at one level of analysis (e.g. individual IS use) influence changes at another level of analysis (e.g. organizational IS use).

IS behavioral research has also been characterized by different sets of ontological and epistemological assumptions (Orlikowski and Baroudi 1991), as well as assumptions regarding the goal of theory (Gregor 2006). Positivist IS research assumes that objective reality exists, and that knowledge of such objective reality can be obtained by applying scientific methods. Therefore, positivist researchers seek to uncover such objective reality in the form of underlying social and technical laws or regularities that can help predict future events. Consequently, positivist research studies are usually evaluated in terms of their ability to make conclusions about the underlying objective reality using such criteria as construct, statistical, internal and external validity. In contrast, interpretive researchers assume the existence of multiple socially constructed, subjective realities that can only be understood from the perspectives of individual actors. The goal of interpretive research is to gain understanding of events from the perspective of different parties involved. The evaluation of interpretive research is based on such principles as hermeneutic circle, contextualization, interaction between the researchers and subjects, abstraction and generalization, dialogical reasoning, multiple interpretations and suspicion (Klein and Myers 1999).

The goal of critical research is to reveal contradiction and conflict in the existing social order (Orlikowski and Baroudi 1991); hence, critical research studies need to be evaluated based on their ability to critique the existing status quo by drawing on core concepts from critical social theories, taking a value position and challenging the existing social practices, and transform the social order through individual emancipation, improvements in societies and improvements in social theories (Myers and Klein 2011). Whereas the positivist research has traditionally dominated the IS discipline (Orlikowski and Baroudi 1991), the interpretive and critical approaches received considerable attention in the 2000s.

The design science paradigm is rooted in engineering, and is usually concerned with the design, development and evaluation of new artifacts and approaches (Hevner et al. 2004; Gregor and Jones 2007). The goal of design science is to create innovations. Design science is not a substitute for behavioral research. Instead, behavioral and design research can co-exist and supplement each other (Hevner et al. 2004). Design research typically seeks to address some of the issues identified in behavioral research by proposing new technological or methodological solutions (Markus et al. 2002). In the recent years design science approach has received renewed attention in the IS academic community.

IS theories, frameworks and methods continues to be an important research theme, accounting for 10–15 percent of publications. As new theories and frameworks are introduced and evaluated, this theme is likely to retain a strong presence in IS research (Fig. 2.2).

Instrument Development and Validation: The idea of construct operationalization and measurement is deeply rooted in the positivist research tradition. With the goal of scientific research seen as uncovering universal laws governing the domain of study (Kerlinger and Lee 2000), researchers seek to create abstractions of

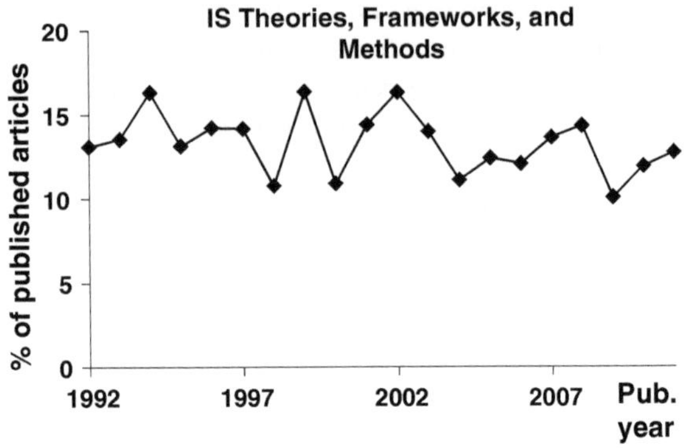

Fig. 2.2 Trends for IS theories, frameworks, and methods

reality using theoretical constructs, and then evaluate such systems of abstractions through theory testing. The pinnacle of theory testing is the ability of researchers to relate theoretical constructs to observable variables, and to measure such variables using measurement instruments. Consequently, an empirical test of a theory is only as good as the operationalizations of the theoretical constructs used in the study. This makes the issue of instrumentation validation and development inseparable from that of methodological rigor. Hence, the quest for rigor in the IS discipline was associated with an increased emphasis on instrument development and validation. Instrument validation typically precedes (conceptually and temporally) the assessment of internal and statistical conclusion validity (Straub 1989). Measurement instruments are typically evaluated in terms of reliability and construct validity, including face, content, discriminant, convergent, and criterion related validity (Kerlinger and Lee 2000; Boudreau et al. 2001).

Research streams in instrument development include construct development methodology (Straub 1989; Lewis et al. 2005), comparison studies between instruments, evaluations of existing instruments, suggested instrument extensions, enhancements, and development of scales for key constructs. Examples of instrument development and validation research include studies conducted to validate scales related to commonly used constructs such as user information

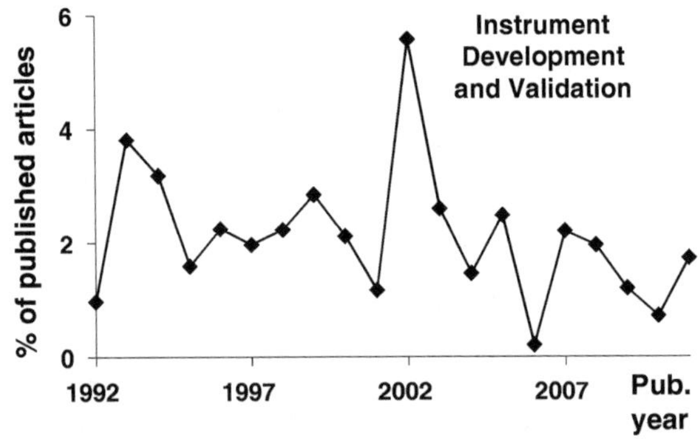

Fig. 2.3 Trends for instrument development and validation

satisfaction (Doll et al. 1995), information resource management (Lewis et al. 1995), information privacy (Smith et al. 1996) and individual trust in online firms (Bhattacherjee 2002). Measuring service quality received particular attention in IS research. Following the original introduction of the SERVQUAL instrument in 1990s (Pitt et al. 1995; van Dyke et al. 1997), its applicability has been explored in the many diverse areas of IT management (Jiang et al. 2002; Yang et al. 2005).

Research in instrument development and validation saw an increase in activity post-1992 as focus on methodological rigor increased. Since then, activity has remained relatively flat (Fig. 2.3).

Chapter 3
IT Artifact and IS Development

In spite of concerns, on the part of some IS academics, about the "missing IT artifact", we find that a major segment of IS research is devoted to the design and development of the various information systems and IT artifacts. Several IS development topics are concerned with IS development methodologies and practices, including system development methodologies, object-oriented approaches, and error detection and management. Other IS development research topics, such as algorithm and program design, data management and database design, modeling techniques and approaches and decision modeling, are concerned with issues common to different types of IS. Finally, some topics are focused on a particular type of IT artifacts and applications, such as business analytics and data mining, intelligent agents, decision support systems, expert systems, and rule-based systems. Some of the topics lie at the intersection of IS development and other areas of IS research. For example, research on networks includes studies on digital as well as social networks, and systems development methodologies research incorporates organizational and behavioral issues. In the next sections, we provide a brief overview of the research topics that are most closely related to the IT artifact and IS development.

3.1 IS Development Methodologies and Issues

Systems Development Methodologies: Systems development methodologies are frameworks that provide structure to the software development process. While numerous types of methodologies exist (e.g., agile, iterative, prototype, waterfall, etc.), each offers a formalized plan and ensures that key steps in the development process are completed. The use of systems development methodologies is often cited as a way of improving the quality of software as well as increasing the likelihood of successful implementation.

IS academicians have sought to categorize and explicate the philosophical underpinnings of various systems development methodologies. Hirschheim and

A. Sidorova et al., *A Survey of Core Research in Information Systems*,
SpringerBriefs in Computer Science, DOI: 10.1007/978-1-4614-7158-5_3,

Kleinim (1994) observe that systems development methodologies often take a functionalist perspective and argue for the inclusion of emancipatory principles embodied by the neohumanist philosophy. Kendall and Kendall (1993) view various aspects of systems development methodologies from a metaphorical perspective, noting that the Systems Development Life Cycle (SDLC), for instance, draws upon the "game" metaphor. The authors argue that this perspective sheds new light on systems development methodologies and that individuals who have a deep understanding of this metaphorical view are better able to conceptualize strengths, weaknesses, and possible combinations of methodologies. Finally, Iivari et al. (1998) argue that IS development methodologies are driven by IS development approaches. The authors compare and contrast several approaches and offer a framework for paradigmatic analysis based on ontology, epistemology, methodology, and ethics.

Much research has been focused on issues such as adoption and use of development methodologies (Fitzgerald 1998). Research suggests that managers are generally more positive about systems development methodologies than developers (Huisman and Iivari 2006). Moreover, perceptions of methodologies differ among the two groups, with managers focusing on issues of alignment, productivity, and quality, and developers focusing on support for verification and validation. Some studies suggest that instead of outright rejection of systems development methodologies, developers tailor the methodologies to suit the needs of the particular development effort (Fitzgerald 1997).

Effects of SDM use on project outcomes have been widely researched. Some findings suggest having some methodology is generally better, in terms of improving the economic success of software development projects, than having none at all (Chatzoglou 1997). Others point to potential negative consequences associated with the use of some methodologies. For instance, Beath and Orlikowski (1994) argue that inconsistencies related to the assignment of responsibilities during the software development process can create tension between users and the software development team. More recent research suggests that project quality is determined by the interplay of multiple factors including the use of a methodology (agile methodology), project control and requirements change (Maruping et al. 2009b).

In spite of the emergence of new methodologies, systems development methodology research as a percentage of published articles has fallen steadily over the past two decades. This suggests research opportunities exist related to the emergence, use and adoption of the new methodologies (Fig. 3.1).

Object Oriented Approaches: Object-oriented design is the process of designing a system by defining the objects which capture both the data structure and the behavior of an information system. Object-oriented (OO) development is characterized by such principles as data abstraction, encapsulation, modularity, polymorphism and inheritance. Object-oriented systems have been analyzed and studied in a variety of problem domains including hypermedia (Lee et al. 1999), hospital administration (Deng and Fuhr 1995), and managing web traffic (Lai 2000). Major research streams in the area of object-oriented approaches are

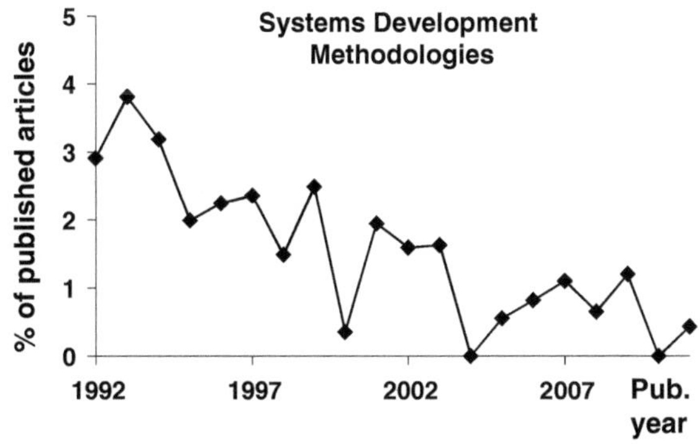

Fig. 3.1 Trends for systems development methodologies

developer training and system design principles, design techniques and approaches, and database design.

One of the major challenges in OO design is the partitioning of the problem and definition of the objects. Several studies have been conducted on object definition and partitioning (Jones et al. 1998) and there have been several attempts of formalizing the OO design process (Liang et al. 1998; Wang 1996). Research has also been conducted to evaluate post-design performance of OO database systems and generic benchmarking tools have been proposed (Darmont and Schneider 2000). Research revealed the importance of matching OO methodologies with OO tasks and process-oriented methodologies with process-focused tasks (Agarwal et al. 1996).

OO approaches have been examined in relation to their compatibility with traditional relational database management systems (RDBMS) (Deng and Fuhr 1995), as well as maintaining system integrity in OO applications implemented to span geographically dispersed sites (Purao et al. 2002a, b). Work on object-oriented database (OODB) systems includes the design of graphical techniques for representing OODB designs (Bradley 1992) and the design of an interface layer on top of an OO storage repository to provide both a level of abstraction above the data and acceptable performance (Jung-Ho and Kim 2002).

Following the introduction of object-oriented techniques, a major concern centered around the transition of developers who were trained on structured development methodologies to the new OO methodologies. Research findings point to a rather straightforward transition between methodologies: after receiving the appropriate training, developers and designers do not have to unlearn structured programming in order to be effective with OO methodologies (Shaft et al. 2008).

Research on object-oriented design and approaches peaked during the early to mid-1990 as the technology gained in popularity. However, as object-oriented design became more common, research interest waned and research on object-oriented approaches has steadily fallen (Fig. 3.2).

Error Detection and Management: Error detection and management research has covered a wide range of areas including spreadsheet development, training, software development, speech recognition systems, and query languages. Major

Fig. 3.2 Trends for object oriented approaches

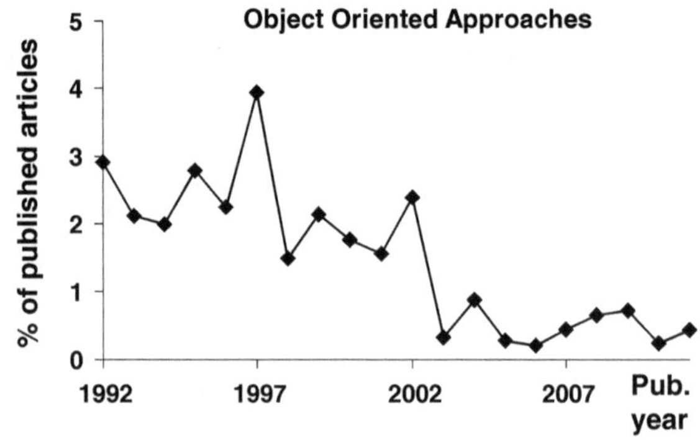

research foci include causes of errors, prevention and avoidance, and detection and correction.

Errors in spreadsheet, software products, and other applications can lead to considerable losses for businesses. It has been estimated that spreadsheet errors alone may cost organizations millions of dollars annually (Powell et al. 2009). Some of the factors that have been found to lead to errors include developer inexperience, poor design approaches, application type, problem complexity time pressure and the lack of review procedures (Janvrin and Morrison 2000).

Studies on error avoidance found that teams with high team members' satisfaction with the group activity often outperform individuals when it comes to error avoidance (Panko and Halverson 2001). In software development, maintaining a balance between software construction and testing can reduce not only the number of errors generated, but also the overall project cost (Ji et al. 2005). Software development is more efficient when the developer's mental representation of the system is consistent with the mental representation of the planned enhancement (Shaft and Vessey 2006). Several studies have investigated error avoidance in query formation. Research found that object-oriented query languages perform better than relational query languages (Wu et al. 1994), restricted natural language query languages can perform better than keyword based query languages for novice users (Suh and Jenkins 1992), and the use of visual query languages as compared to textual query languages reduces mental workload and errors in complex tasks (Speier and Morris 2003).

Humans are typically weak in error detection. However, giving individuals explicit goals to find errors and incentivizing them accordingly significantly improves their error detection rate (Klein et al. 1997). Exposing trainees to errors during training also significantly enhances their error recovery skills (Sein and Santhanam 1999). Visualization tools can aid in error detection and correction during spreadsheet development (Goswami et al. 2008). However, errors in a spreadsheet can be discovered more effectively in a printed version of the spreadsheet as opposed to a version displayed on a computer screen (Galletta et al. 1997).

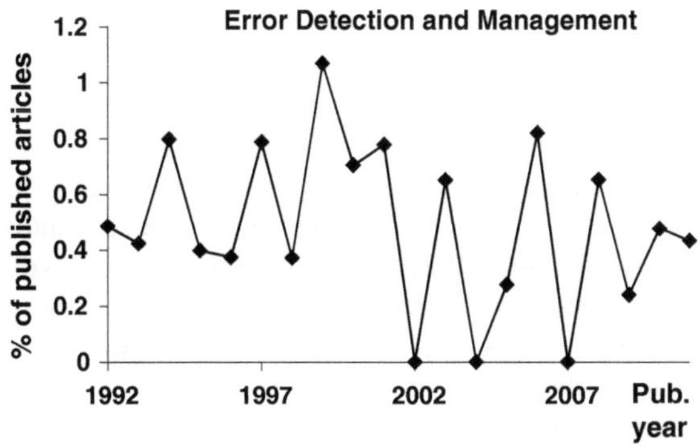

Fig. 3.3 Trends for error detection and management

Research in the area of error detection and management has continued at a somewhat steady pace over the past two decades. The amount of research has been sparse, accounting for less than 1 % of the articles published annually (Fig. 3.3).

3.2 Modeling and Design of IS

Modeling Techniques and Approaches: Conceptual models are used to create a representation of an application domain independent of any system implementation. The goal of the conceptual model is to create a representation that aids in the understanding of the problem domain (Bera et al. 2010). Descriptions of phenomena within the target domain are created using a well-defined grammar (Parsons 2011; Soffer and Hadar 2007). Conceptual schemas (i.e., maps of concepts and their relationships describing the semantics of the domain) and ontology languages (i.e., a representation of the concepts within a domain and relationships defined through a shared vocabulary and taxonomy) serve as a means by which a conceptual model is constructed. Some view the two as related and argue that conceptual schemas should utilize grammars based on the theory of ontology and incorporate ontological semantics into their representation (Zhang et al. 2007). Others suggest that the two are epistemologically different and should be used as complimentary modeling techniques (Fonseca and Martin 2007). Still others have raised concerns over the fundamental theoretical foundations upon which the conceptual modeling grammars are based (Parsons 2011).

Research on modeling techniques and approaches also covers such issues as: language development, model evaluation and analysis, multi-model representations and integration, and model extensions. Language development research has focused on improvements of techniques and approaches to enhance the descriptive capabilities of the models. Examples include the use of philosophical ontological properties to guide the development of ontology languages (Bera et al. 2010) as well as using the psychology of language to develop new psycho-linguistic structures (Evermann 2005).

Work in the area of model evaluation and analysis has included the use of metamodel-independent algorithms to identify mappings and differences between different model representations (Lin et al. 2007), and the use of the good decomposition models (GDM) to explore the descriptive power of a given model (Burton-Jones and Meso 2006). Differences between models were studied from a semantic perspective of introducing vagueness into the mapping process (Hadar and Soffer 2006). Research has explored lower level constructs and issues such as those related to explicit property precedence (Parsons 2011) and the use of the part-of construct in conceptual modeling (Shanks et al. 2008). Model extensions such as the extension of the Unified Modeling Language (UML) to include information related to spatiotemporal data (Price and Jensen 2000) have also been proposed. The integration and reconciliation of multi-model representations has presented a challenge to researchers, especially in the presence of multiple modeling techniques (Joosten and Purao 2002).

The amount of research in the area of modeling techniques and approaches has slowly dropped from about 2.5 % in the 1990s, to about 1.5 % of the articles published in the 2000s. However, the number of published articles appears to have stabilized in recent years (Fig. 3.4).

Decision Modeling: Research in decision modeling explores techniques used to guide the computer-aided decision making process. The research has traditionally focused in two areas: individual and group decision making. In individual decision making the goal is to evaluate and rank alternatives to a given problem. In group decision making, the opinions of multiple decision makers or stakeholders must be reconciled. Challenges facing decision support systems and decision modeling include large search spaces of potential solutions, the presence of multiple criteria, incomplete or unavailable information, understanding the context of the problem space and adjusting for potential inconsistencies or conflicts.

In the area of individual decision modeling multiple criteria decision analysis (MCDA) methods have been used to cluster and rank potential alternative solutions (Henggeler et al. 1994). Attempts to improve rankings have included even swap methods (i.e., an elimination method based on trade-offs) (Li and Ma 2008),

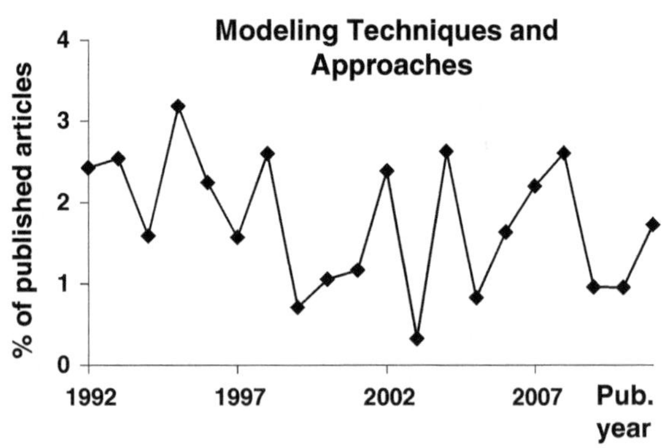

Fig. 3.4 Trends for modeling techniques and approaches

use of decision maps to visualize the information (Comes et al. 2011), fuzzy set theory (Lin and Hsieh 2004), and generic algorithms (Fazlollahi and Vahidov 2001).

Group decision modeling involves aggregation of preferences of several individuals, whose opinions may vary, and carry different weights. Within this context, alternatives must be evaluated and ranked and ultimately used to help guide the decision maker to a solution. Studies have focused on algorithms that attempt to minimize differences (Contreras 2011), weighted pairwise decision matrices using scales that measure the potential impact of alternative solutions (Ribeiro et al. 2011), and distance-based group decision-making methods (Yu and Lai 2011).

Decision modeling research has covered diverse problem areas including software development (Ribeiro et al. 2011), tenant selection and property management (Yau and Davis 1994), and portfolio and financial management (Lin and Hsieh 2004). Since a peak in mid-1990s, research into decision modeling has dropped off significantly and hovered around 0.5–2 % of the articles published (Fig. 3.5).

Algorithms and Problem Solving: Information systems play an important part in supporting problem solving activities. Structured problem solving is achieved through the systematic application of formal procedures in order to perform a calculation and arrive at a solution. These sets of rules for problem solving are called algorithms and, in the context of IS, are typically embedded in a computer system. The creation and evaluation of new algorithms, as well as the exploration of the problem solving process are important themes in IS research. Theoretical approaches for general types of problems have been offered, such as the design theory nexus approach for solving ill-structured or "wicked" problems (Pries-Heje and Baskerville 2008).

Unlike programming-focused algorithm design research in computer science, algorithm design research in information systems tends to be problem focused. Examples include the problem conceptualization for service priority selection for grid computing services users (Lin and Lin 2006), algorithm development for problems related to the acquisition of network resources (Kasap et al. 2007), and software development optimization (Dawande et al. 2008). Many of the algorithm

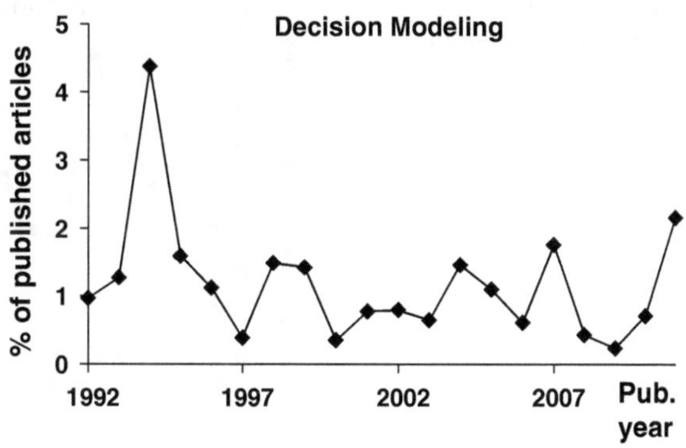

Fig. 3.5 Trends for decision modeling

design research efforts are associated with the development of decision support systems (hence, overlap with the DSS topic).

In addition to algorithmic support, IT provides information, presentation and communication support of problem solving activities. Beginning with seminal papers such as Von Hippel's (1994) research on information stickiness, numerous studies have examined information as a key input of the problem solving process. Human factors have been shown important determinants of problem solving process and outcomes. Individual user characteristics, such as DSS expertise (Lee et al. 2008) and contextual knowledge (Lee 2004), were shown to play an important role in problem solving.

Algorithm and problem solving research has decreased over time. However there is overlap between this type of research and research related to business analytics and data mining. Semantics, rather than material differences in research focus, may differentiate the two research streams. As business analytics and data mining research has increased in recent years, the overall trend associated with algorithm and problem solving research may be more stable than it appears by looking at this topic alone (Fig. 3.6).

Data Management and Database Design: Enterprise data stores contain supplier, customer, and operational data, which are important inputs to organizational decision making processes. Enterprise data and its management have been widely studied in IS. Data management broadly encompasses the storage, organization, security, governance, and retention of enterprise data. Database Management Systems (DBMS) provide support for many data management objectives.

Database modeling and design techniques are critical to database design. In addition to extending and examining commonly used entity-relationship model approaches to database modeling (Balaban and Shoval 1999), researchers have proposed new approaches to data modeling (Booch 2000). Other examples of research include the design of early semantic database prototypes as a method for user validation of conceptual database models (Baskerville 1993) and the development of methods for detecting and explaining referential integrity errors (Ordonez and García-García 2008).

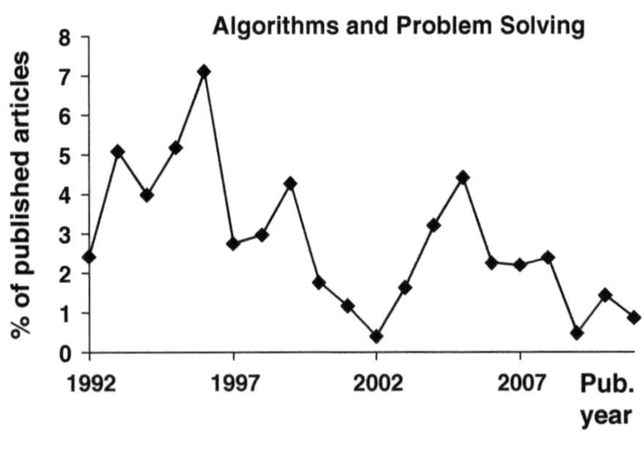

Fig. 3.6 Trends for algorithms and problem solving

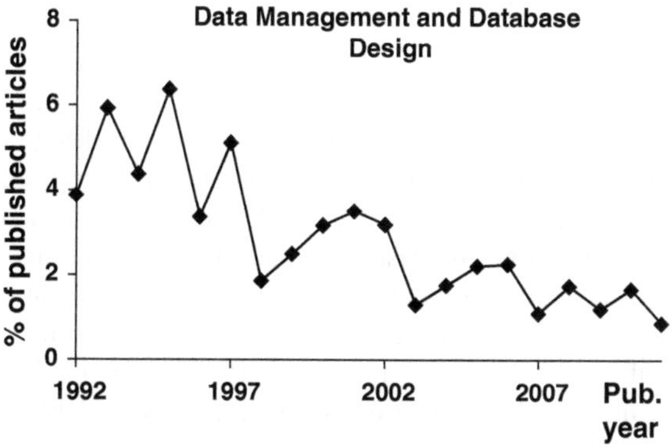

Fig. 3.7 Trends for data management and database design

Data retrieval represents another important stream of research associated with data management and database design. Research focusing on database queries is prolific and addresses topics ranging from mining queries to optimize database performance (Chen et al. 2003) to query relaxation techniques to facilitate approximate answers (Shin et al. 2008).

Much of the data management literature is associated with the management of multiple databases. Whether each database is unique or is a part of a larger distributed system, management of data across data stores is challenging. Studies proposed and evaluated graphical user interfaces for interacting with multiple databases (Tan et al. 1998), and interfaces to facilitate data retrieval, such as the model for natural language queries in multiple database environments in which query context is not required (Ein-Dor and Spiegler 1995). Other research focused on techniques for integration of disparate database systems (Lim and Chiang 2004).

Other important themes in data management research include database performance and use optimization (Seng et al. 2005; Konana et al. 2000), and data security (Weippl et al. 2003).

Data management and database design research has fallen over the last 20 years. This downward trend is likely related to the maturity of the associated technologies as well as a shift in focus to the study of less-structured data management objectives such as knowledge management and content management (Fig. 3.7).

3.3 Design of Specific Types of IT

Decision Support Systems: Decision support systems (DSS) are computer based systems that aid decision makers in finding solutions to problems. Often the problems are complex and underspecified and the DSS must utilize data models and analytical techniques to derive potential solutions (Sprague 1980). Multiple DSS models have been suggested and discussed including symbiotic, expert, holistic and adaptive (Mirchandani and Pakath 1999). Research in the area of DSS is fragmented (Eom et al. 1993) and covers many diverse areas. Some of the main streams of research focus on assessing system effectiveness and benefits, defining methods of measuring effectiveness, system design considerations and studies on derivative systems and applications in specific problem domains.

Research into DSS benefits has explored such outcomes as decision quality, cost reduction, increased productivity, time savings, and whether or not the systems provide a competitive advantage (Udo and Guimaraes 1994). Other outcomes of interest include relative use, perceived utility, output satisfaction and goal realization (Kivijarvi and Zmud 1993), perceived usefulness, ease of use, enjoyment, overall satisfaction (Pearson and Shim 1994), reduction in uncertainty, and increase in trust (Kayande et al. 2009). Alignment and calibration of DSS has been shown to be an important factor in DSS success (Kasper 1996). For example, the alignment of mental models of the system with that of the user results in uncertainty reduction and an increase in trust (Kayande et al. 2009).

On the DSS design front, stored models (data and decision modules) and metagraphs have been proposed as means of clearly represent the organization (Basu and Blanning 1994). The use of different formulations of problems and solving those simultaneously has been proposed as a mechanism for solving complex problems (Barkhi et al. 2005). The use of fuzzy sets and generic algorithms has also been shown to lead to promising results when generating alternatives in DSS (Fazlollahi and Vahidov 2001).

Derivative DSS have been suggested to improve results. Enhancing DSS through dynamic adaptation to the problem and problem context has shown promising results and led to Adaptive Decision Support Systems (ADSS) (Fazlollahi et al. 1997). Utilizing Socratic dialectic inquiry to better deal with unstructured complex problems led to the Dialectic Decision Support System (DDSS) (Jarupathirun and Zahedi 2007) and utilization of adaptive avatar designs led to ADR-DSS (Chang Lee and Kwon 2008).

Research in the area of DSS has covered many diverse application domains ranging from transportation project management (Barfod et al. 2011) to medical applications (Leroy and Chen 2007). Work in this area reached a peak in the early 1990s and has since been on a downward trend (Fig. 3.8).

Expert Systems: Expert systems are artificial intelligence systems which attempt to solve problems through processes which mimic the reasoning of human experts. Such systems are based on a set of rules, the knowledge base, which are used by the system to arrive at decisions. Expert systems have a long history of research by IS academics. Research streams related to expert systems include new development or expansion of expert system capabilities, knowledge extraction from human experts, and expert system use and guidance for practice.

The knowledge base at the heart of expert systems contains a series of IF … THEN rules that enable the system to reason. The acquisition of these rules requires knowledge elicitation from human experts. This is an often difficult and imperfect process, and is best viewed as an inquiry in which expertise is created, not simply extracted from experts (West 1992). Due to the complexity of this

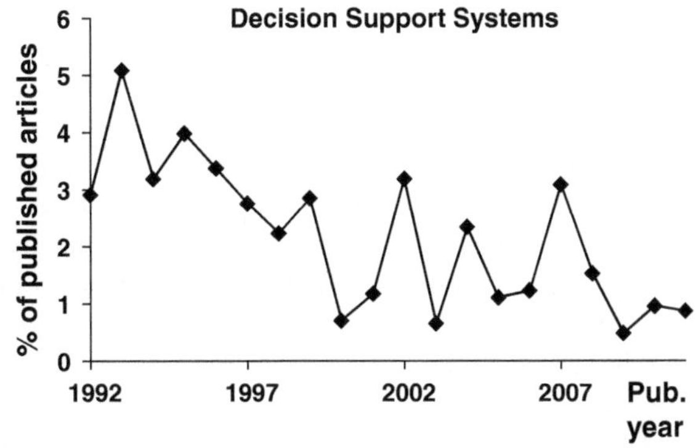

Fig. 3.8 Trends for decision support systems

process, IS research identified and evaluated a variety of knowledge elicitation techniques and methods, from the use of group decision support systems (Liou and Nunamaker Jr. 1993) to repertory grid and Delphi methods (Chiravuri et al. 2011).

IS researchers have devoted considerable attention to developing new types of expert systems and enhancing expert system capabilities. Synergistic expert systems consisting of multiple expert systems working in concert were designed to allow solving problems that are too complex for a single expert system (Beeri and Spiegler 1996). The combination of rule-base expert systems with stochastic models was proposed to improve decision making with semi-structured data (Lenard et al. 1998). Hyper-media enabled expert systems with higher media richness were shown to improve both knowledge acquisition and transfer to users (Tung et al. 1999).

Surveys of expert system use in business have found that expert systems are lightly used and often abandoned due to managerial issues (Gill 1995). The successful implementation and continued use of expert systems has therefore been extensively studied. Research sought to identify factors influencing successful development, implementation, and organizational adoption of expert systems (Yoon et al. 1995), and the utilization of expert system recommendations (Ye and Johnson 1995).

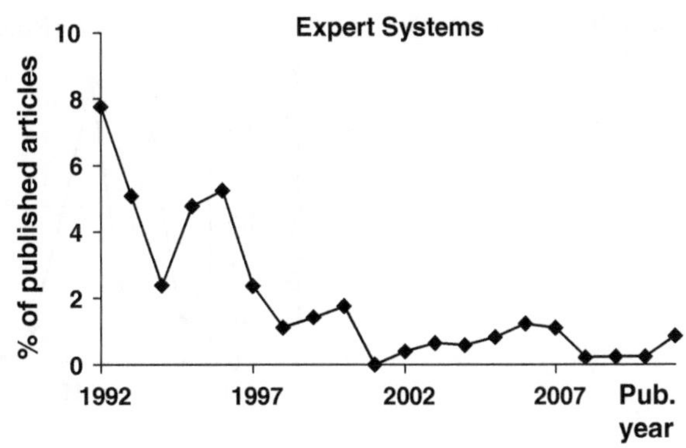

Fig. 3.9 Trends for expert systems

Expert systems research has fallen precipitously over the last 20 years from almost 8 % in 1992, to around 1 % in 2000s (Fig. 3.9).

Rule-Based Systems: A rule is a principle which provides formal guidance for conduct. In the context of information systems, two aspects of organizational rules are of importance. First, rules are often prolific and must be managed. Second, rules must be interpreted and applied. Rule-based systems enable the storage, management, and interpretation of rules, typically to facilitate some type of decision-making process. The most recognizable example of rule-based systems in information systems is the expert system. IS research related to rule-based systems can be divided into two categories: rule base research and inference engine research.

The rule base (also referred to as the knowledge base) contains the list of rules the system must interpret. As the rule base tends to be extremely complex (Higa 1996), research is concerned with rule base management issues. These include identification of essential and redundant rules (Hammer and Kogan 1996) and organization of rules within the rule base. Because a greedy inference engine will select the first rule encountered which satisfies the criteria, even if more specific and better fitting rules exist in the rule base, system performance can be improved by generating rule orders which allow better solutions to be found first (O'Leary 1997). As exhaustive rule base validation and verification procedures can be computationally expensive and/or resource prohibitive, research efforts have been extended towards finding new approaches to validation and verification (Chander et al. 1997).

The application and interpretation of rules is the domain of the inference engine. Inference engines are often required to perform defeasible reasoning, in which rules are not entirely consistent and conclusions are acknowledged to be fallible. The automation of such reasoning is a highly complex task, and IS research offers theoretical and empirical solutions (Geerts et al. 1994).

Rule-based systems research displayed an upward trend through the mid-1990s, declined in the late 1990s and stabilized at about 0.3 % of articles in the 2000s (Fig. 3.10).

Business Analytics/Data Mining: Business analytics and data mining are concerned with the detection of interesting patterns in large organizational data

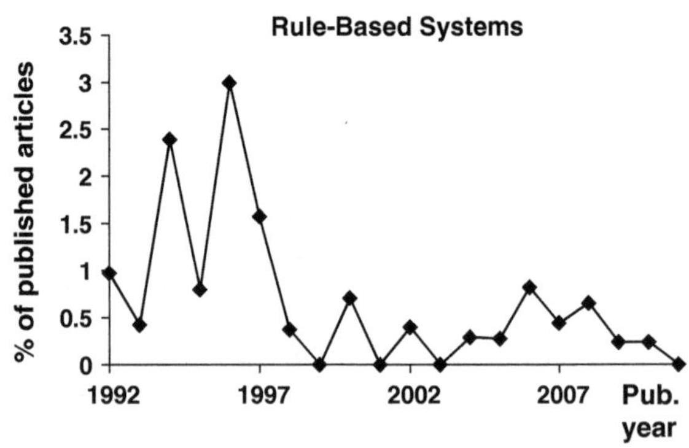

Fig. 3.10 Trends for rule-based systems

sets through the application of data management and analysis techniques, statistical analysis, modeling, and artificial intelligence. Analysts using these techniques typically attempt to identify, classify, model, and report data patterns in terms of actionable information for improved decision-making. In the business context, both approaches are often used for the development of improved customer understanding. Business analytics typically involves a priori hypotheses and is focused on analysis of data to prove or disprove these suspected relationships. In contrast, data mining is discovery-focused, using analysis to uncover patterns without preconceived notions of what might be found.

Business analytics and data mining research often seek to develop new methods to improve performance over existing approaches. Examples of studies include research on the inclusion of domain knowledge into data mining classifiers (Sinha and Zhao 2008), top-down mining of sequential patterns (Liu et al. 2010a), and decision-centric data acquisition (Saar-Tsechansky and Provost 2007).

Another stream of research within this topic area attempts to evaluate and compare techniques in the context of a specific analytical challenge. Examples include the study of performance measures for the comparison of data mining techniques (Sinha and May 2005), the examination of the optimal training set size for neural network forecasting, and the application of the Kohonen self-organizing map technique to textual classification (Lin et al. 2000).

Business analytics and data mining studies typically validate the efficacy of methods by applying the analysis approach in the context of a business problem. Such analysis is often focused on prediction of future outcomes and typically applied to financial concerns (Bose and Mahapatra 2001). Common topics include financial fraud detection (Ngai et al. 2011), corporate credit rating analysis (Huang et al. 2004), and bankruptcy prediction (Wilson and Sharda 1994).

Business analytics and data mining research increased steadily over the last 20 years. This topic accounted for almost 6 % of research published in 2011 and is among the top 5 topics in IS research based on articles published between 1992 and 2011 (Fig. 3.11).

Information Search and Retrieval: The expansion of the information available within corporations and on the Internet drives the need for more effective and

Fig. 3.11 Trends for business analytics/data mining

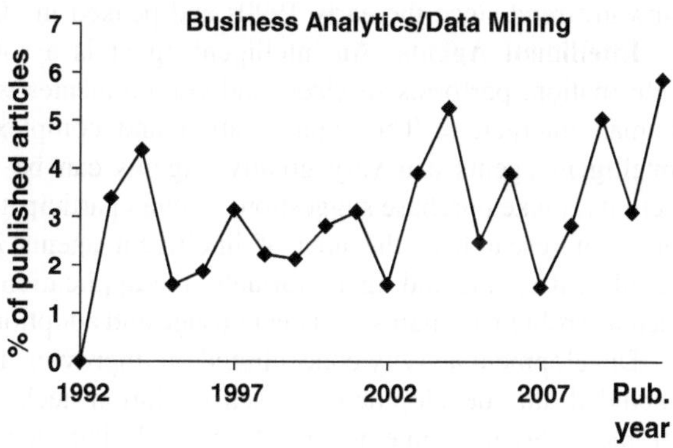

efficient search techniques. As the information volume and diversity continues to grow distinguishing between relevant and irrelevant information becomes increasingly difficult (Chau and Chen 2008). Current search engines are fast in terms of their response time, but often the relevance of the search results is lacking (Fan et al. 2005).

Much of the research in information search and retrieval has concentrated on search engine optimization. Another area of interest is document and database retrieval. Within the area of search engine optimization some of the major focus areas include improved search performance, ranking and clustering and multilingual and image searching.

Many techniques have been explored to improve search performance. Adapting existing search techniques with perception indices that utilize fuzzy logic (Choi 2003) and incorporating dynamic adaptive intelligent agents (Menczer 2003) have both resulted in improved performance. Context-aware query refinement through the construction of a semantic also net has been shown to improve performance (Storey et al. 2008).

Clustering techniques have been developed using graph theory to better identify document similarities and associations (Boley et al. 1999). Improved ranking functions have been developed that use generic programming and incorporate both content and structural information (Fan et al. 2005). Ontology concepts have been employed to refine ranking and re-rank documents to enhance search relevancy (Kayed et al. 2010).

Traditional search engines have been adapted to cover multilingual content (Zhou et al. 2006). Techniques for rapid language identification have been proposed in order to improve subject-categorization (Prager 2000), and latent semantic indexing has been used to enhance multilingual document retrieval through the construction of knowledge maps (Wei et al. 2008).

In the area of database retrieval, flexible storage and indexing techniques have been used to support complex queries without the need for reformatting of the source data (Sengupta and Venkataraman 2011). In document retrieval systems generic algorithms together with matching functions have been used to improve document retrieval (Fan et al. 2006).

Research in the area of information search and retrieval has shown a positive upward trend since the early 1990s and peaked in 2003 (Fig. 3.12).

Intelligent Agents: An intelligent agent is a software program that gathers information, performs services, and communicates with other agents, all without human interaction. The sophistication and complexity of what are considered intelligent agents can vary greatly. Agents can be used to track web-browsing activity, make purchase suggestions or even participate in negotiations. Three main areas of research in the area of intelligent agents include: the development of intelligent agents and agent variants, the application of intelligent agents in particular problem domains, and agent usage and adoption (Wang and Benbasat 2005).

Development activity concentrated on improving agent tasks effectiveness. This included the development of self-evolution techniques, which allow agents' problem-solving strategies to develop during deployment (Meng and Pakath

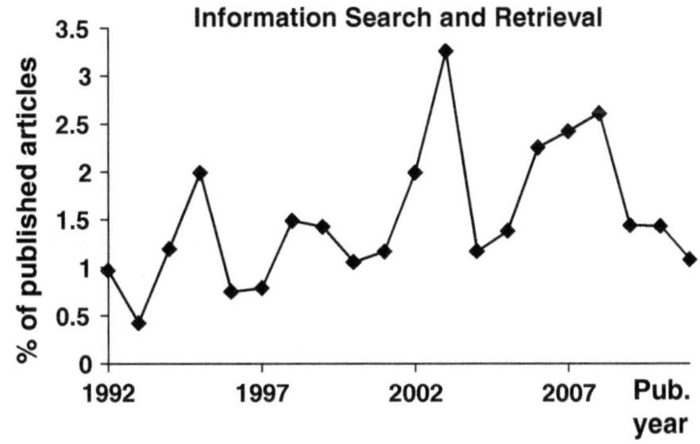

Fig. 3.12 Trends for information search and retrieval

2001), as well as agent collaboration approaches that enable agents to work together (Pendharkar 2007).

Intelligent agents have been used in the development of decision support systems (DSS) for different types of decision tasks (Bui and Lee 1999), in healthcare systems to aid healthcare professionals managing patient care (Meng and Pakath 2001), in production scheduling (Pendharkar 2007) and supply chain management (Kim and Cho 2010), and in psycho/physiological analysis of human responses (Nunamaker et al. 2011). Web-based applications are one of the larger areas of use of intelligent agents. Intelligent agents are used in web-based, mobile and e-commerce applications for interactive negotiations, point-of-sale comparison shopping (Moukas et al. 2000) and as recommendation agents (Wang and Benbasat 2005).

Research in the area of intelligent agents first experienced a spike in 1997, was strong in the late 1990s through mid-2000s, but declined in the late 2000s (Fig. 3.13).

Networks: In the broadest sense, a network can be defined as a system of interconnected nodes. Using this definition, it is clear that numerous network types are relevant to the study of information systems. IS has a long history of research on telecommunications and digital networks, and these remain an important part of the

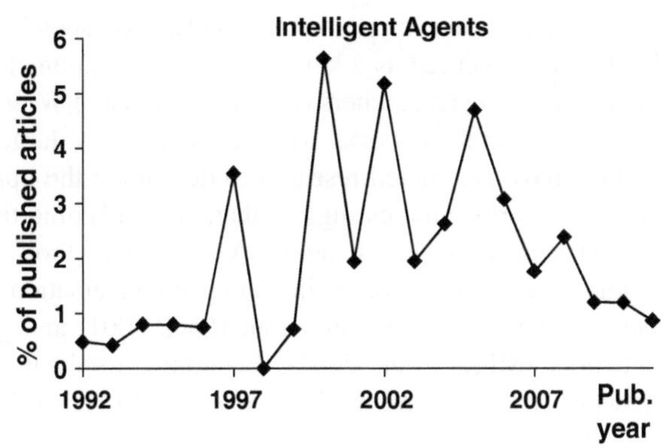

Fig. 3.13 Trends for intelligent agents

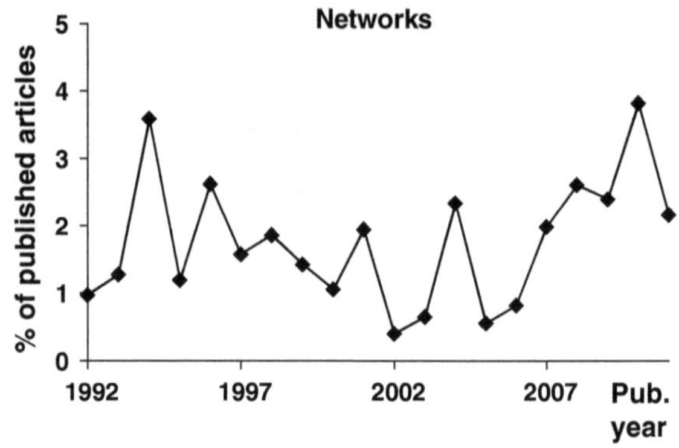

Fig. 3.14 Trends for networks

networks research stream. In addition, significant IS research has been directed at topics related to artificial neural networks, and in recent years, social networking.

Telecommunications and digital networks are fundamental components of the infrastructure which supports business information systems and a significant body of IS literature exists on the topic. For instance, Bakos and Nault (1997) examine the drivers and implications of network ownership, concluding, among other things, that sole ownership is preferable when a network participant is indispensable to an asset essential to all participants. Absent this condition, joint ownership is preferred. Kauffman et al. (2000) investigate participation in joint networks and determined that network size and positive network externalities induce early adoption while firm size negatively influences the probability of early adoption.

Artificial neural networks involve the use of artificial neurons which are linked together and can be trained for prediction, classification, or other types of data analysis. Neural networks research addresses methodological issues related to the use of neural networks, such as the use of self-organizing maps as a tool for clustering and demonstrate their effectiveness in this capacity (Kiang et al.1995), the creation or evaluation of neural network algorithms (Sexton et al. 2004), and applications of neural network technologies to specific research contexts, such as financial predictions (Walczak 2001).

Enabled by telecommunication networks, social networking sites (e.g., Facebook) have emerged as a key medium of communication and attracted significant attention among researchers (Parameswaran and Whinston 2007). Given the ability of online social networks to reach extremely large numbers of people, many authors have conducted research to determine the upper bound or optimal size of social networks. Studies suggest that, at some point, the costs of increased network size may outweigh the benefits. A number of tools for social networking facilitation have been proposed, including a conversation map interface for the facilitation of large-scale conversations (Sack 2001) and generic data model for social networks (Mitra et al. 2007). Economic implications of the growth of social networks have also been widely examined (Mayer 2009).

Overall, the volume of network research has remained fairly stable over the last 20 years. The composition of these papers has also shifted over time, with the focus moving away from electronic networks to social and neural network topics (Fig. 3.14).

Chapter 4
IT and Organizations

Organizational use of IT and the effect of IT on organizational practices and outcomes are widely researched in the IS community. One stream of organizational IS research deals with organizational consequences of IT, such as the effect of IT investments on firm value, and the role of IT capabilities in gaining competitive advantage. The second stream deals with organizational IT use and management topics such as organizational adoption of IT, IS planning and strategic alignment, control and IT architecture, outsourcing and labor sourcing, the use of open source software, and IS security and risk management. The third stream of research is focused on specific classes of organizational IS, such as electronic data interchange, supply chain management and enterprise resource planning systems, or executive information systems. Finally, the fourth stream is focused on the social context of organizational IS use and includes such topics as e-government and cultural issues in IS. In the next sections, we provide a brief overview of organizational IS research topics.

4.1 Organizational Consequences of IT

IT Investments and Firm Value: Researchers have been striving to better understand whether or not IT investment directly or indirectly impacts firm value. A number of studies examined the impact of IT investment and IT innovation on corporate valuation, productivity, targeted cost reduction, market dynamics, and organizational efficiency. Results have been mixed illustrating the complexity of the problem.

In-depth investigations of the phenomenon suggest that the type of the IT investments matters. For example, IT infrastructure investment is perceived by the investment community as a platform for growth and results in positive abnormal returns and an increase in trading volume (Chatterjee et al. 2002). Similarly, announcements of investments in innovative technology have a positive impact on the value of a firm, while average technology investments have zero net present value (NPV) (Dos Santos et al. 1993).

A. Sidorova et al., *A Survey of Core Research in Information Systems*, SpringerBriefs in Computer Science, DOI: 10.1007/978-1-4614-7158-5_4,

Studies of the impact of IT investment on productivity rendered inconsistent results. Some of the conclusions point to the need to consider IT investments in combination with the associated non-IT investments (Ko and Osei-Bryson 2004). For example, changes in employee composition coupled with IT investments can differentially impact productivity: decreases in the proportion of clerical and professional staff coupled with IT investments were found to be associated with an increase in productivity, while a reduction in managerial personnel coupled with IT investment led to reduction in productivity (Francalanci and Galal 1998).

IT investments that target fixed cost reduction have been found to lead to improved productivity and profitability while those targeting variable costs may improve profitability in the short-term, but lead to a decrease in long-term productivity (Thatcher and Oliver 2001). Research also shows that focused technology investments (e.g., introduction of ATM's in the banking industry) can lead to improved profitability of the firm (Ou et al. 2009).

The timing of technology investments is also important. Early adopters of technology gain the most benefit in terms of competitive advantage as compared to late adopters (Weill 1992). In addition, the development, deployment and training time involved in adding IT infrastructure may cause a delay in realized benefit to the firm. In other words, IT investment may indeed show a positive return, but that return may come over a longer payback period (Kivijärvi and Saarinen 1995).

Research exploring the relationship between IT investment and Firm Value has been somewhat sporadic over the past two decades, accounting for 1–4 % of publications (Fig. 4.1).

IT Capabilities and Firm Performance: Related to the issue of IT investment impact of the firm value is the question: do IT capabilities positively influence firm performance? IT capabilities and firm performance are often examined through the theoretical lens of the Resource Based View of the Firm (RBV) and researchers have examined the phenomena in terms of both general IT capabilities and specific technology solutions.

The term "resource based view" was popularized by Birger Wernerfelt in his 1984 article "A Resource-based view of the Firm" and was further developed in a series of articles by Jay B. Barney. RBV posits that a firm can achieve and sustain

Fig. 4.1 Trends for IT investments and firm value

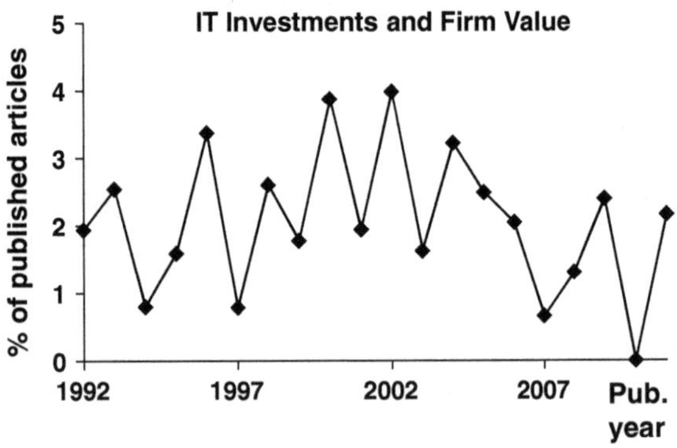

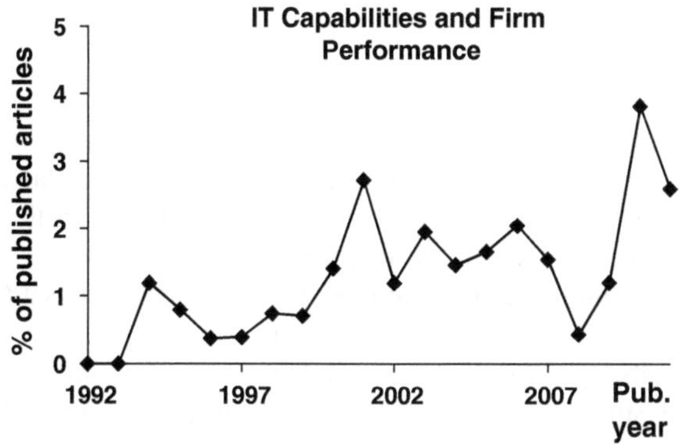

Fig. 4.2 Trends for IT capabilities and firm performance

a competitive advantage based on its use of resources which are valuable, rare, in-imitable, and non-substitutable. Applying RBV to IT suggests that IT capabilities may be viewed as an organizational resource which is related to firm performance (Mata et al. 1995). In support of the theory, a highly cited study of IT capabilities and firm performance found that firms with high IT capability exhibit better overall profit and cost-based performance than those with low IT capability (Bharadwaj 2000).

Not all IT capabilities equally influence firm performance. A study of three types of organizational IT capabilities: value, competitive, and dynamic found that competitive capabilities such as relationship infrastructure and dynamic capabilities such as organizational learning impact competitive advantage but value capabilities such as the quality of IT infrastructure do not (Bhatt and Grover 2005).

Several studies examined specific technology solutions and their impact on firm performance. Organizational use of knowledge management systems was shown to contribute to dynamic capabilities critical to firm performance (Sher and Lee 2004). E-commerce has been shown to increase firm performance when aligned with existing infrastructure capability (Zhu and Kraemer 2002; Zhu 2004).

IS research related to IT capabilities and firm performance has risen over the last two decades. After declining in late-2000s, IT capabilities and firm performance research has seen a strong resurgence in recent years (Fig. 4.2).

4.2 Organizational IS Use and Management

Diffusion of Innovation: The organizational adoption of IS is an important topic for both practitioners and academics. Much of the organizational IS adoption literature characterizes technology as beneficial innovations which serve to improve organizational performance, and thus views organizational IT adoption as the diffusion of innovation. Guided by Rogers' Diffusion of Innovation (DOI) model (Rogers 1995) diffusion innovation research offers considerable insight into determinants of organizational adoption.

Rogers' DOI model suggests that, due to variations among individual potential adopters, innovation adoptions over time follow the normal distribution. Based on their position in the normal distribution adopters are classified into innovators, early adopters, early majority, late majority, and laggards. Four innovation characteristics positively influence its adoption: relative advantage, compatibility, trialability, and observability. A fifth characteristic, complexity, has a negative impact on the rate of adoption.

Building on the DOI model, Moore and Benbasat (1991) identified eight factors which affect the rate of IT adoption: relative advantage, compatibility, trialability, visibility, ease of use, result demonstrability, image, and voluntariness. A number of studies examined effects of additional IT-related factors on the IT adoption process. For instance, price was found to be an important determinant of adoption (Tam 1996). Perceptions about technology's critical mass in the market were found to influence organizational disposition to adoption (Van Slyke et al. 2007).

Several studies examined the role played by organizational and contextual factors in technology adoption. Environmental uncertainty and decentralized decision making were shown to be significantly related to organizational technology adoption (Grover and Goslar 1993). Organizational characteristics such as information processing requirements were shown to positively affect the rate of adoption (Melville and Ramirez 2008). A study of diffusion of innovations among European firms found that innovation characteristics (compatibility, security concerns, and cost) and contextual characteristics (technology competence, partner readiness and competitive pressure) significantly impact organizational adoption (Zhu et al. 2006).

While much of the literature views innovation as desirable, innovation diffusion can be viewed as a disruptive force which may spur new innovations while at the same time disturb existing organizational IT strategy (Lyytinen and Rose 2003). Baskerville and Pries-Heje (1998) acknowledge potential negative consequences of diffusion of technology innovation and conceptualize positive barriers to DOI.

Diffusion of innovation research has remained relatively stable over the last two decades, representing between 4 and 5 % of publications (Fig. 4.3).

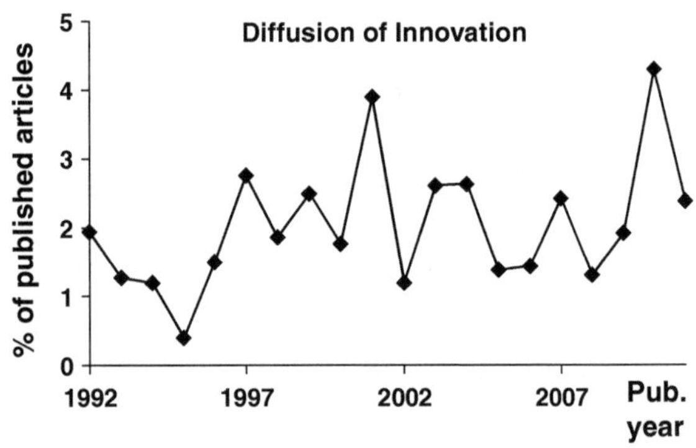

Fig. 4.3 Trends for diffusion of innovation

Strategic Information Systems Planning: Comprehensive Strategic Information Systems Planning (SISP) is a critical activity for modern organizations. The aim of SISP is to ensure that information systems are used in a manner consistent with organizational objectives through the selection and prioritization of changes to an organization's IS resources. Because the goal of SISP is to create an IS plan that is in alignment strategic goals of the business, SISP requires involvement of both technical and functional managers. IS research on SISP focused on the planning process itself, planning quality, and the alignment of IS and organizational objectives.

Multiple approaches to SISP exist and such approaches often evolve over time (Grover and Segars 2005). SISP is influenced by a number of organizational and contextual factors. Organizations that view IS as critical to their success commit more resources to the planning process and establish longer planning horizons (Premkumar and King 1992). Business change (but not IT change) has been shown influence SISP planning horizons (Newkirk et al. 2008).

The quality of plans produced as a result of SISP generally improves as organizations mature and adopt more formal planning processes (Cerpa and Verner 1998). Planning resources, the intended strategic impact of IS on future business operations, the quality of facilitation mechanisms, the quality of implementation mechanisms, and the quality of strategic business planning have all been demonstrated to significantly impact the quality of strategic planning (Premkumar and King 1994). Several tools have been suggested to facilitate the creation and management of strategic IS planning including Group Support Systems, Decision Support Systems, and balanced scorecards.

The alignment of IS objectives and strategic organizational goals has received considerable attention in the IS literature. Despite its importance, strategic alignment remains an elusive objective (Pavri and Ang 1995). Several important determinants of alignment have been identified. Shared domain knowledge, strategic business plans, IT implementation success, communication between business and IT executives, and connections between business and IT planning have been shown to impact short-term alignment, whereas shared domain knowledge and strategic business plans influence long-term alignment (Reich and Benbasat 2000). Related to the shared domain knowledge business competence of the IS executives was found to be an important factor in achieving business-IS alignment (Teo and King 1997).

Strategic information systems planning research boomed in the 1990s but declined in the 2000s (Fig. 4.4).

Control: In the context of information systems, controls generally refer to policies, structures, or actions which serve to ensure that behaviors (either system or human) are aligned with organizational goals. Controls may be formal (e.g., rules, regulations, and organizational policies) with explicit punitive consequences for violations and formalized rewards for compliance, or informal (e.g., customs, norms, and culture) which often have social consequences. IS research on controls is varied, however three prominent research streams may be observed: studies on

Fig. 4.4 Trends for strategic information systems planning

IT project management controls, studies related to inter-organizational controls, and studies which propose tools to facilitate control design or implementation.

IT project management is a complex task and often involves the coordination of numerous groups in order to ensure successful project completion. IT project management controls are often complex and include both formal and informal controls, some of which may be overlapping and redundant (Kirsch 1997). Controls often evolve over time as the project progresses through different phases (Kirsch 2004). Evolution of controls was also observed in outsourced software development projects (Choudhury and Sabherwal 2003). Much of the research on controls in IT project management deals with requirements volatility in software development projects. Research suggests that volatile requirements in the context of agile software development methodologies are best addressed by allowing development teams "controlled" autonomy. Outcome controls which specify the desired project outcome allow teams to stay focused on achieving their objective while allowing autonomy to address the changing requirements (Maruping et al. 2009).

Controls in inter-organizations business transactions represent another important topic of research. The nature of data exchanged between business partners is shown to influence the use of controls. In the EDI context, the mix of controls used and their efficiency vary based on the type of EDI application, with financial applications favoring automated controls and trade applications making better use of formal controls (Lee et al. 2005). Characteristics of the relationship between business partners, such as the level of trust, have also been shown to influence the use of controls (Gallivan and Depledge 2003).

Several tools for control design, implementation, or management have been proposed, including tools for modeling inter-organizational controls (Kartseva et al. 2010) and workflow solutions for improving coordination and management of business processes (Kumar and Wainer 2005).

IS control research has trended slightly upward over the last two decades, however it has been extremely volatile. Overall, this research stream accounts for less than 1 % of IS research, but it has surpassed that threshold in several peak years (Fig. 4.5).

Fig. 4.5 Trends for control

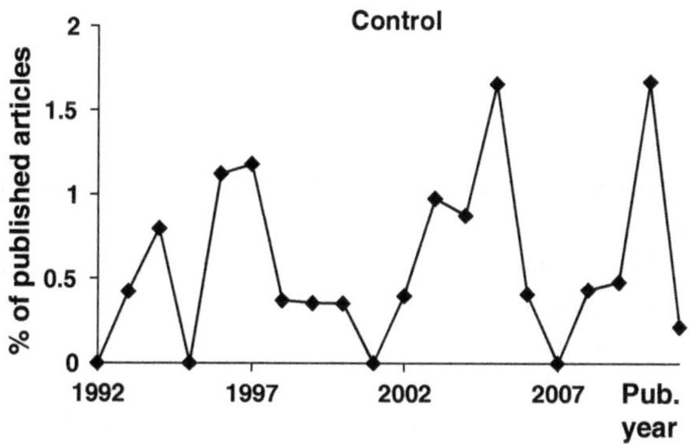

IS Risk Management: IS risk management involves the identification, assessment, and prioritization of risks which may result in negative impacts to information systems projects. After identification and triage, risk management practices seek to control outcomes through risk avoidance or mitigation strategies. Information systems projects experience high rates of failure and some suggest that improved risk management processes may help reduce the failure rate.

The development of successful management strategies depends on understanding the intricacies of what is to be managed. Numerous studies seek to identify the types of risks encountered on IS projects. Results of a multi-country Delphi method study suggest that the lack of top management commitment to the project is the top ranked risk among experienced project managers in Hong Kong, Finland, and the United States (Schmidt et al. 2001). The study also offers a list of 50 IS project risks in 14 categories. The composition of project risks is influenced by the characteristics of a project. A study of risks in onshore and offshore development contexts suggest that some risks appear in both contexts, some appeared in both contexts but are exacerbated in the offshore context, and some are unique to offshore development projects (Nakatsu and Iacovou 2009). Prominent risks associated with high risk projects also differ from those associated with medium and low risk projects: requirements risk, planning and control risk, and organizational risk are most prominent for high risk projects while complexity is most prominent for low risk projects (Wallace et al. 2004).

IS research has shown that individual characteristics alter perceptions of risk. End user perceptions of project risk differ from those of IS managers (Keil et al. 2002), and manager's perceptions are in turn different from those of senior executives (managers focus primarily on operational risks and executives focus on more strategic risks) (Liu et al. 2010b). Experience level and perceived control has also been demonstrated to alter perceptions of risk (Du et al. 2007).

A number of risk management strategies and techniques exist, and research suggests that for optimal performance the risk management profile must fit the risk exposure of the project (Barki et al. 2001). Unfortunately, IS managers often address risk management intuitively, without reliance on formal models (Benaroch et al. 2006). A study by Lyytinen and Mathiassen (1998) highlights similarities and differences between four important risk management approaches, including McFarlan's portfolio approach, Davis' contingency approach, Boehm's software risk approach, and Alter's and Ginzberg's implementation approach. The authors encourage managers to gain a deeper understanding of each strategy and to be prepared to construct hybrid approaches to better meet their risk management needs.

IS risk management research has steadily risen over the past 20 years, although it still accounts for less than 2.5 % of published research (Fig. 4.6).

IS Security: Information system security covers a wide range of areas including security policies, risk analysis and management, contingency planning and disaster recovery (Von Solms et al. 1994). Given rapidly changing business and market conditions, security policies must adapt and keep pace if the organization is to remain secure (Siponen and Iivari 2006). The area of information security has both a technical and a behavioral component. Often, it is the employee that is viewed as the weakest link in keeping information secure (Boss et al. 2009). Some estimate that between 50 and 75 % of all security issues originate within the firm (D'Arcy et al. 2009). Although, most of the attention focuses on the business environment, it must be recognized that security is an issue in the home where over a billion users may be connected to the internet and often remotely to their offices (Anderson and Agarwal 2010).

Some of the main research streams in the area of IS security include adherence to security policies, value to the firm, and trade-offs related to the implementation of security protocols.

Security breaches are not always intended to be malicious in nature: employees often underestimate the risk (Herath and Rao 2009) or do not perceive themselves as security risks and simply adhere to existing workgroup norms (Guo et al. 2011). Security policy education, including employees in the information security process and fear appeals have been found to improve adherence to security policies (Boss et al. 2009; Spears and Barki 2010; Johnston and Warkentin 2010). Certainty of detection has been shown to encourage adherence to security policies but research on the severity of sanctions has led to inconsistent findings (D'Arcy et al. 2009; Guo et al. 2011).

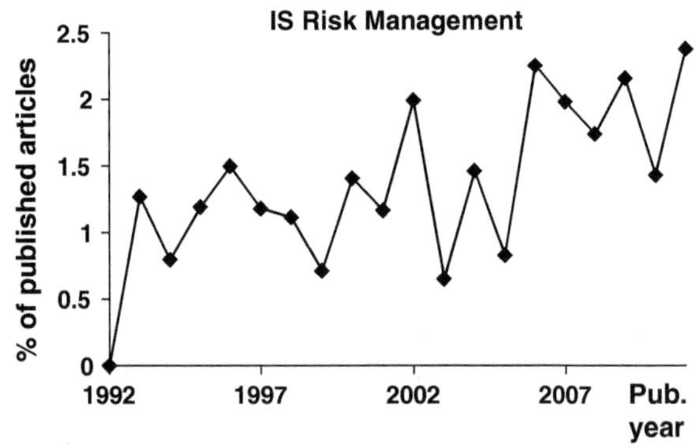

Fig. 4.6 Trends for IS risk management

Research indicates that implementing IS security measures can enhance firm value. Voluntary SEC disclosure regarding information security readiness appears to positively impact firm value (Gordon et al. 2010). Public announcement related to security measures has been shown to improve firm value through abnormal market returns (Chai et al. 2011) and to deter attacks (Cremonini and Nizovtsev 2010).

Often implementation of IS security involves tradeoffs in terms of economic costs and benefits, business opportunities, and productivity. Companies must find a balance between minimizing security infrastructure expenses and providing the maximum amount of protection (Gupta et al. 2006). The value-at-risk approach focusses on estimating the level of risk and making security investment decisions matching the risk exposure and risk profile (Wang et al. 2008). Pursuing business opportunities may be associated with IS security risks, and companies must find a way to addresses such security risks while fully leveraging the new market opportunities. Researchers have explored frameworks for modeling market transactions and environments, services within the market, and security measures to find the appropriate balance (Röhm and Pernul 2000).

The volume of research in IS security has been steadily increasing. Research peaked in 2009, accounting for more than 4 % of the published articles (Fig. 4.7).

Software Development and Use (Packaged and Open Source): Computer software (SW) lies at the core of most information systems. Research in the area of software development and use is diverse, ranging from software marketing to development processes and quality. A major area of interest has emerged around the impact of open source software (OSS).

OSS is software developed in loosely coupled virtual communities of skilled developers who work together to produce, often high quality software (Ljungberg 2000) that is made freely available to the community at large. What began as a group of individuals freely contributing their skill and effort to an open community has grown into a source of commercially viable technology (Fitzgerald 2006). The open source movement has played a significant role in the transformation of segments of the software industry, and the competition between open source solutions, commercial versions of open source, and commercial solutions emerged

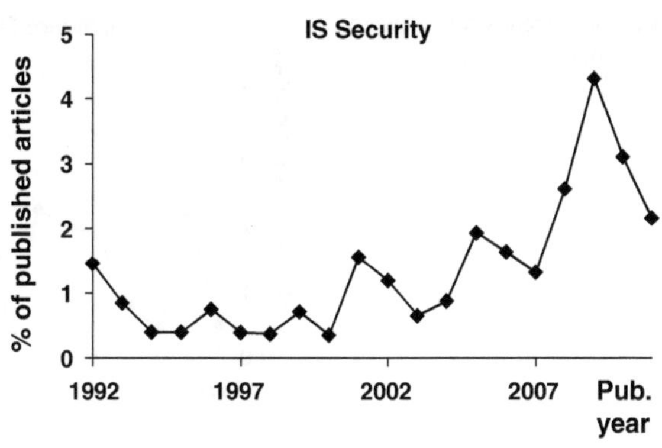

Fig. 4.7 Trends for IS security

as an important theme in software development research (Raghu et al. 2009). The benefits for firms looking to adopt OSS include the low cost of solutions, a vast support network and source code access (Goode 2005). The concerns include perceived low reliability and accountability with respect to support, a substantial learning curve, potential incompatibility with other existing systems (Goode 2005), potentially restrictive licenses (Subramaniam et al. 2009) and security (Payne 2002).

Project management has been another area of interest within SW development research. Key research issues include project budgeting, scheduling, expectation management (Lind and Sulek 1998), development processes (Xu and Ramesh 2007), quality control, and the economics of defects and defect resolution (Westland 2004). With the rise of alternative development approaches, use of such approaches (e.g., extreme programming practices) to address challenges encounter during the development process and the relationship between software structure and maintenance costs have also been explored (Banker and Slaughter 2000).

In the software use domain, much of research has focused on buy versus build decisions, as well as the choice of software upgrade versus switch decisions (Castner and Ferguson 2000). Other areas of research have included software piracy (Peace et al. 2003).

Research in software development and use has exhibited an upward trend, peaking with over 4 % of the total publications in 2008 (Fig. 4.8).

Outsourcing and Labor Sourcing: Outsourcing is the process of externalizing a business function or process by contracting with an outside service provider. Outsourcing may entail anything from provisioning support for an individual production application, to contracting for the entire IT function. The rationale for outsourcing varies but it is commonly pursued in order to allow an organization to focus on core competencies and reduce costs. In 2000s and 2010s, outsourcing has become a key management tool and is commonly utilized in the context of IT. Key areas of research include the outsourcing decision-making process, impact of client-provider relationships, and the management of outsourcing engagements.

Cost reduction is often cited as a major outsourcing driver and numerous studies have examined outsourcing from this perspective (Ang and Straub 1998).

Fig. 4.8 Trends for software development and use

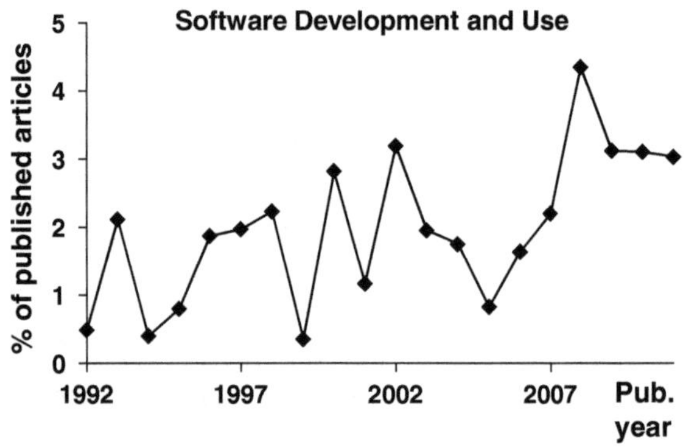

Companies that have lower cash reserves, higher debt, or declining growth employ outsourcing seeking to generate cash and reduce costs (Smith et al. 1998). However, the motives for outsourcing are complex, interrelated, and cannot be distilled down to cost reduction alone (Baldwin et al. 2001). For instance, CEO rewards may influence the introduction of outsourcing and therefore managerial self-interest may be a factor (Hall and Liedtka 2005). In addition, both internal and external factors, including corporate strategy, have been shown to influence the decision to outsource and the selection of functions for outsourcing (Barthélemy and Geyer 2005).

A number of studies examined the various aspects of client-provider relationships and their impact on outsourcing outcomes. Outsourcing providers are often viewed as strategic partners (Willcocks and Kern 1998) and informal relationship management structures are an important channel through which vendors share value (Levina and Ross 2003). Participation, communication, information sharing, and top management support all positively influence partnership quality, while age of relationship and mutual dependency have a negative influence (Lee and Kim 1999).

The management of outsourcing projects is another important area of research. Maintaining flexibility to respond to the dynamic business environment is critical to the successful management of outsourcing (Tan and Sia 2006). Contract management, in particular, has received considerable attention in the literature. Contracts may be used to both encourage and discourage vendor behaviors and it is important that managers have a good knowledge of contract types (Bryson and Ngwenyama 2000). Completeness of outsourcing contracts is also of importance as incomplete contracts may result in underinvestment and inefficient bargaining (Susarla et al. 2010).

After a period of volatility during the late 1990s, outsourcing research rose steadily towards a peak in 2010. While 2011 showed a decrease in outsourcing research, it is likely to remain an important research area (Fig. 4.9).

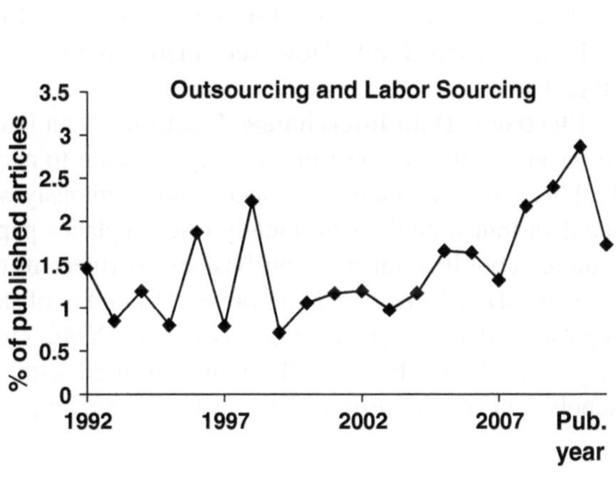

Fig. 4.9 Trends for outsourcing and labor sourcing

4.3 Classes of Organizational IS

Enterprise Resource Planning Systems: Enterprise resource planning (ERP) systems integrate information, both internal and external, across an organization covering multiple functional areas. The goal of an ERP system is to facilitate the sharing and flow of information between the different functional groups as well as to outside stakeholders (Bidgoli 2004).

ERP systems hold the promise of a wide range of organizational benefits, yet determining the value of an ERP system to an organization is often difficult (Osei-Bryson et al. 2008). Although ERP system investments positively impact firm value over the long-term, often the short-term impact is minimal (Hitt et al. 2002). Assessing the value of investment is also complicated by the fact that the return comes more in terms of strategic rather than operational value (Stefanou 2001).

With about three quarters of ERP implementations failing to meet expectations (Wu et al. 2007), a large segment of ERP literature focuses on ERP implementation critical success factors, and reasons for implementation failures (Karimi et al. 2007). ERP Systems tend to be complex and expensive to implement. System complexity, together with cultural issues as well as technical issues have impacted adoption and deployment. Some of the factors positively influencing successful ERP deployment include: strong commitment from leadership (Staehr 2010), organizational contexts (Gattiker and Goodhue 2005), open communication and empowered implementation teams (Sarker and Lee 2003).

Organizational and national culture plays an important role in the success of ERP implementations. Several studies examined culture-related issues such as cultural misfit between the country of implementation and country of origin of the ERP (Wang et al. 2006), the impact of organizational culture on corporate communication (Nah et al. 2007), and the effects of ERP systems on organizational culture (Ke and Wei 2008). At the individual level, the use of ERP systems has been examined from a variety of perspectives, including effort-performance expectancy, performance-outcome, outcome valence (Lim et al. 2005), uncertainty avoidance, and other perspectives.

Research on ERP emerged in the 1990s, peaked in the 2005–2007 timeframe, and then dropped off. However, there continues to be interest in the topic (Fig. 4.10).

Electronic Data Interchange: Electronic Data Interchange (EDI) is the transfer of business information from one organization to another in an electronic format. EDI processes are intended to operate autonomously without human interaction and the data transmitted electronically often replaces paper-based transmissions. EDI requires coordination between business partners in order to ensure that the data exchanged can be read and interpreted. A number of standards have been adopted to regulate both data formats (e.g., ANSI X.12, XML, etc.) and transmission protocols (e.g., HTTP, SOAP, etc.). EDI is widely used with manufacturing processes and supply chain functions in which a customer exchanges data with a materials supplier.

Fig. 4.10 Trends for enterprise resource planning systems

EDI adoption research suggests that organizational readiness, external pressure, and perceived benefits are significant predictors of EDI adoption (Iacovou et al. 1995). Organizational decision to adopt EDI is also influenced by technological, organizational, and inter-organizational factors Chwelos et al. (2001).

Research into partner relationships and their effect on EDI use suggests that partnership attributes such as trust, interdependence and commitment significantly influence an organizations' willingness to implement EDI (Lee and Lim 2005). EDI partner selection is driven a number of factor including strategic commitment, EDI infrastructure, communications, etc. (Angeles and Nath 2000). The use of EDI is sometimes imposed upon suppliers by a customer champion: In such cases, EDI is seen as a strategic necessity by suppliers, and strong customers employ both "carrot" and "stick" to encourage adoption (Barua and Lee 1997). While both the customer champion and forced adopters may see some benefit from EDI use (Lee et al. 1999), forced adopters may not see the same level of benefit as champions (Rao et al. 1995). This may be due, in part, to forced adopters not fully utilizing EDI capabilities (Tuunainen 1998).

Research interest in EDI peaked in the late-1990s but dropped precipitously in the 2000s (Fig. 4.11).

Supply Chain Management: The supply chain (SC) is defined as a network of firms involved in the upstream and downstream flow of products, services, finance,

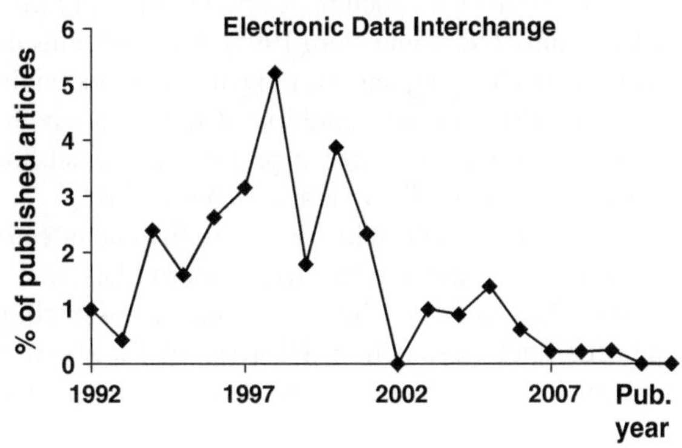

Fig. 4.11 Trends for electronic data interchange

and information needed to deliver a product to the end consumer. Supply chain management (SCM) is a term that is used in the literature to refer to the flow of material and products within a system in operational terms and the management of the flow of a distribution channel from supplier to consumer (Mentzer et al. 2001).

Research has largely concentrated on the value of facilitating communication and sharing information, creating digitally connected enterprises throughout the SC (Levermore et al. 2010). The major research streams include analysis and optimization of the SC in order to improve corporate performance, and simulation and modeling of the supply chain.

The effective management of the SC has become a point of strategic value and importance for most firms (Malhotra et al. 2007). Research points to the importance of enhanced communication between partners for improving firm performance. The availability, quality and timeliness of information shared throughout the SC is shown to lead to positive returns, while poor quality or inaccurate information has negative consequences (Legner and Schemm 2008). Improved visibility throughout the SC aids in reconfigurability which improves firm performance (Wei and Wang 2010), reduces transaction costs, and enhances SC flexibility (Gosain et al. 2005). Creating information flow between partners allows each participating company to better manage their collective assets and as a result be more adaptive to changing market conditions (Malhotra et al. 2007).

Modeling and simulation of the SC has enabled companies to improve analysis and enhance overall performance. Multi-agent models have been used to predict and resolve fulfillment conflicts within the SC (Lin et al. 2008). Agent-based demand forecast simulation has aided in improving inventory management, reducing costs, and smoothing order variation (Liang and Huang 2006).

The volume of SCM research has shown a steady increase since 1996, and was particularly high in late 2000s (Fig. 4.12).

Executive Information Systems: An executive information system (EIS) is often thought of as a special purpose decision support system (DSS) (Westland 1992). EIS are intended for use by executives within an organization to access information relevant to management activities (Leidner and Elam 1994).

Early EISs were considered high-risk systems with more system implementations resulting in failure than success (Rainer and Watson 1995). Executive decisions often lack structure, leverage informal information, rely on intuition, and lack certainty (Nord and Nord 1995). Early systems lacked the flexibility needed to adapt to the changing and ever expanding work environment. As systems evolved they expanded to access multiple data sources both within and outside the corporation and became better at performing the ad hoc analysis needed to support changing demands (Cheung and Babin 2006).

Approaches to enhancing the flexibility and effectiveness of EIS include the use of repositories and model-driven approaches that facilitate the integration of multiple data sources (Chen 1995), the use of intelligent multi-agent architectures and neural networks (Chi and Turban 1995), as well as mapping the EIS closer to strategic business objectives and strategic management process (Singh et al. 2002).

Fig. 4.12 Trends for supply chain management

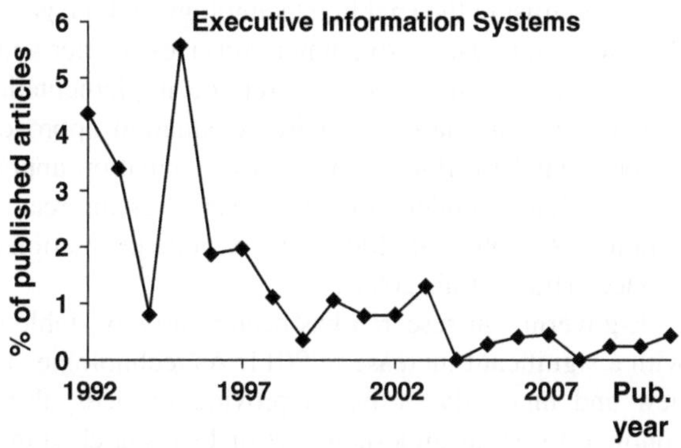

Fig. 4.13 Trends for executive information systems

Research on EIS use and outcomes suggests that EIS utilization is influenced by experience, organizational norms, user satisfaction, the level of access and assistance, and perceived value delivered by the EIS (Bergeron et al. 1995). Regular use of EISs increases problem identification speeds, decision making speed, and depth of analysis in decision making (Leidner and Elam 1994).

Research in the area of executive information systems peaked in the early 1990s and declined sharply in the late 1990s and early 2000s (Fig. 4.13).

4.4 The Social Context of the Organizational IT Use

E-government: E-government is the provision of government information and services to citizens, businesses, and other government agencies using information technology. Besides providing another channel through which these exchanges may take place, e-government seeks to improve service quality through increased efficiency and effectiveness. In addition to the provision of services (e-administration), e-government also includes transformation of political systems (e-democracy), although politicians often foster the former and inhibit the latter (Mahrer and Krimmer 2005). IS research on e-government has explored its transformational nature, adoption, and readiness.

Much in the same way that the Internet and associated technologies transformed interactions with businesses, the provision of services through electronic channels has fundamentally altered interactions with governments. The use of Interned-based technologies has led government institutions to behave in a more entrepreneurial manner (West Jr. 1997) and to view citizens as customers (Mosse and Whitley 2009). The benchmarking of services offered electronically by governments demonstrates the newly developed customer focus.

As governments invest heavily in the transformation to e-government services, it is important to ensure that the intended consumers make use of the new capabilities. E-government service adoption research points to perceived ease of use, compatibility and trust in the enabling technology and the government as good predictors of the intention to use e-government services (Carter and Belanger 2005).

Assessing agency readiness for the implementation of e-government services and investment analysis requires evaluation approaches tailored to the needs of governmental institutions. Proposed evaluation approaches include the e-government readiness model which suggests assessing readiness at strategic, system, and data levels (Koh et al. 2008), and ex-ante evaluation techniques for e-government services (Irani et al. 2005).

E-government research has been relatively stable throughout 1990s and 2000s, with a significant increase in 2011. As technologies mature and governments seek new and innovative ways to provide services, this research stream will likely continue to be an important part of IS research (Fig. 4.14).

Cultural Issues in IS: Culture refers to a set of shared values, beliefs, and assumptions (Hofstede 1991). While core aspects of culture are intangible, culture may be expressed in observable ways such as human behavior and the creation of artifacts. Cultural research in information systems seeks to understand the effect of culture on human interactions with computer systems, their designers, and their users. Building on a comprehensive review of the existing body culture research in

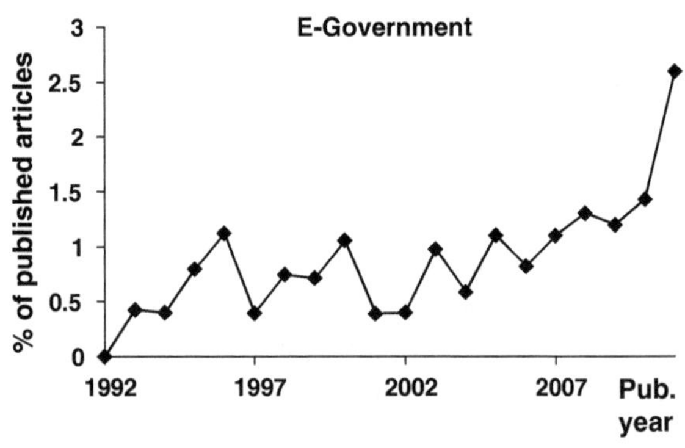

Fig. 4.14 Trends for E-government

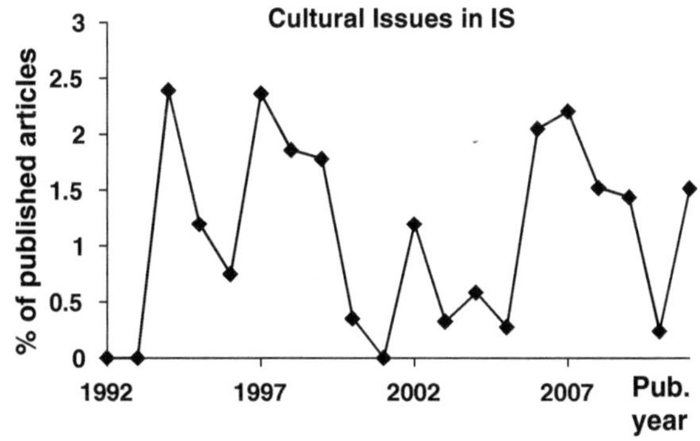

Fig. 4.15 Trends for cultural issues in IS

IS, the theory of information technology culture conflict identifies three cornerstones of IT culture conflict: IT values, group member values and values embedded in IT (Leidner and Kayworth 2006). The aforementioned cultural values and the resulting conflict exist at national, organizational or subunit levels.

The vast majority of cultural research in IS has focused on national culture, often described along five dimensions: individualism versus collectivism, power distance, masculinity versus femininity, uncertainty avoidance, and long-term versus short-term orientation (Hofstede 1980).[1] Research suggests that national culture and economic development influences issues related to organizational IS use and management (Watson et al. 1997), technology adoption and use (Straub 1994), as well as technology outcomes, e.g. satisfaction (Mejias et al. 1997).

Like the national culture, organizational and IT cultures influence IT development, management and use. The influence of organizational culture may be formal or informal and may be reflected in business processes, technologies, and the structure of an organization. Cultural influences are not uniform within an organization and variances in individual values affect the successful use of technology (Alavi et al. 2006). A hierarchical culture, which seeks security, order, and routinization, is common in IT organizations and impacts systems development methodologies (Iivari and Huisman 2007). IT culture was also found to be decidedly masculine in nature (Harvey 1997).

Despite fairly significant year-to-year variation, the overall number of IS culture papers as a percentage of published articles has remained relatively stable (Fig. 4.15).

[1] By measuring these dimensions and ranking countries accordingly, Hofstede established a national culture profile for each country studied. In spite of numerous criticisms, Hofstede's conception of national culture continues to inspire much of the cultural research in IS.

Chapter 5
IT and Individuals

Research of the individual use of IT and the effects of IT on individual behavior and outcomes constitutes the most voluminous IS research area. This area can be broadly subdivided into research on factors in individual adoption and use, and research on personal computing environments. Identification of critical success factors related to the individual use and adoption of IT has been among the prominent research topics. Notably, much of the critical success factors (CSF) research is also concerned with organizational issues; however, because the individual focus is dominant, the CSF topic is reviewed in this chapter. Related to CSF is research on individual IS acceptance and use, research on learning and training, as well as research on privacy issues and trust. Individual level IS research is particularly concerned with three computing environments: end user computing, web-based systems and mobile computing. Finally, individual level IS research includes the topic of IT effect on jobs and that of IT careers. The aforementioned research topics are reviewed in the following sections.

5.1 Factors in Individual Adoption and Use of IT

IS Success Factors: Success in IS is usually studied from one of the three perspectives: individuals' perceptions of system success; IS project team success, and successful organizational use of IS. As expected, the independent variables and the measures of success vary accordingly. The IS Success Model (DeLone and McLean 1992, 2003) provides much of the theoretical grounding for the IS success research.

Predictors of success at the individual level include individual perceptions of the system characteristics (usefulness, ease of use, control, etc.), individual characteristics (e.g., expertise, personality traits, self-efficacy, computer anxiety, etc.), and exogenous factors influencing individual perceptions (e.g., training, management support, task characteristics, etc.). At the individual level, success is often measured in terms of user satisfaction; however, other concepts such as

A. Sidorova et al., *A Survey of Core Research in Information Systems*, SpringerBriefs in Computer Science, DOI: 10.1007/978-1-4614-7158-5_5,

system acceptance, use, perceived quality, and impact on personal performance have been used as proxies for system success. Unlike technology acceptance research, IS success research tends to focus more heavily on use outcomes. System use, therefore, is viewed as a necessary precondition to the recognition of some other success measure. Seminal studies of the individual-level IS success factors include the examination of training, self-efficacy, and performance (Compeau and Higgins 1995), as well as view of success based on the task-technology fit view (Goodhue and Thompson 1995).

At the IS project level, success is often examined in the context of project management and team management. Success is usually measured as adherence to project schedule or budget (Henry et al. 2007), or successful implementation of business functionality. Project management factors which affect project success include project manager performance, managerial involvement and attitudes; project planning, coordination mechanisms, conflict resolution strategy, and development approach. Team characteristics examined in the context of IS project team success include of team skill, trust, and experience. Team composition and, more specifically, user participation in the development process (McKeen et al. 1994) have repeatedly been cited as antecedents of IS project success.

At the organizational level, success is usually measured in terms of positive organizational outcomes such as improvements in firm finance, increased market share, or through the recognition of a new competitive advantage (Santhanam and Hartono 2003). Success is evaluated in relation to specific types of IS, such as ERP and e-commerce systems, or in terms of IS management, including successful organizational use of IT, strategic use of IT (Weill 1992) and the optimal use of IT outsourcing (Han et al. 2008). System characteristics such as system capabilities and system complexity, as well as firm and industry characteristics such as firm size, IS maturity, and competitive pressure, are often cited as antecedents of organizational IS success.

The study of IS success factors represents a fairly large portion of IS research over the past two decades. By paper count, IS success research is the second most researched topic in IS during the period examined (Fig. 5.1).

Individual IS Acceptance and Use: The acceptance of technologies is a significant concern for both businesses which have developed or implemented

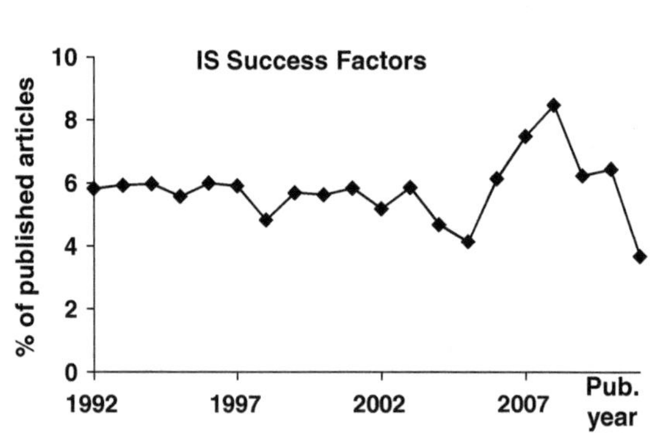

Fig. 5.1 Trends in IS success factors

information systems for internal use and those that market technologies to consumers. While several models and theoretical approaches have been applied to the study of individual IS acceptance and use, the Technology Acceptance Model (TAM) is by far the most widespread. Since its introduction, TAM has been extended several times and both the original model and its extensions have been applied in a wide variety of technology contexts.

Based on the Theory of Reasoned Action (Fishbein and Ajzen 1975), TAM, states that perceptions about a technology's usefulness and ease of use determine an individual's intention to use that technology (Davis 1989). Perceived usefulness and perceived ease of use are among the most highly utilized independent variables in IS research (Jeyaraj et al. 2006). Despite its widespread use, TAM is not without criticism. TAM has been characterized by some as a middle-range theory that accomplished its goal and now serves as a distraction from more significant research problems (Benbasat and Barki 2007). Others have argued that the proliferation of TAM variations has resulted in a lack of a parsimonious view of individual IS adoption (Straub and Burton-Jones 2007).

Numerous extensions to TAM have been proposed, that can be grouped in three categories: inclusion of factors from related models, inclusion of additional belief factors, and inclusion of external variables which are antecedents to, or moderators of, perceived ease of use and perceived usefulness (Wixom and Todd 2005). While numerous examples of studies exist which add one or two new constructs to TAM, two key extensions are of note. TAM2 adds subjective norms as an antecedent to behavioral intention to use; adds result demonstrability, output quality, job relevance, image and subjective norms as antecedents of perceived usefulness; and introduces experience and voluntariness as moderators to the effect of subjective norms (Venkatesh and Davis 2000). TAM2 offers an increase in explanatory power over TAM and provides greater insight into the perceived usefulness construct. Another key extension of TAM research is the Unified Theory of Acceptance and Use of Technology (UTAUT) (Venkatesh et al. 2003). UTAUT describes behavioral intention to use based on performance expectancy, effort expectancy, and social influence. Use behavior is described by behavioral intention and facilitating conditions. Finally, gender, age, experience, and voluntariness of use moderate the relationships between independent and dependent variables. UTAUT has been shown to outperform TAM/TAM2 as well as a number of additional adoption theories commonly employed in IS research.

Individual IS acceptance and use has been studied with numerous technologies. TAM was initially applied to the adoption of e-mail and graphics software by Davis. However, as researchers have modified TAM for various research contexts, the technologies examined with TAM-based models has grown significantly. These studies examine individual adoption phenomena associated with e-commerce (Gefen and Straub 2000), the World Wide Web (Agarwal and Karahanna 2000), and retail online help desk software (Venkatesh 2000). In addition, TAM-based research has been applied to aggregate technology use, as seen in Taylor and Todd's (1995) study of student use of a computing resource center.

Research related to individual IS adoption and use has trended upward for the majority of the past 20 years. The notable exception is a sharp decline between 2006 and 2010 which may be attributable to a certain amount of "TAM-fatigue" within the IS research community. However, 2011 shows an increase over 2010 and given the importance of individual IS adoption, this topic is certain to remain an important part of the IS research agenda (Fig. 5.2).

Trust and Information Systems: In recent years, the concept of trust has garnered considerable attention from IS researchers. Trust, or the willingness of an individual to rely on the actions of another individual or entity, is an important topic in the context of information systems. Information systems regularly serve as mediators for communication or transactions among individuals. The presence of the information system may influence the trust that develops between the individuals involved in the exchange. IS research on trust and information systems is generally focused in two areas: e-commerce and virtual teams.

Trust in the context of e-commerce transactions is complex and multidimensional (McKnight et al. 2002) and a number of authors have attempted to fully define the concept and develop measures for use in research (Bhattacherjee 2002). Perceptions which influence trust, and thereby the decision to engage in e-commerce, may be formed by familiarity with the retailer (Kuan and Bock 2007). Alternatively, perceptions may be developed based on the technological characteristics of the e-commerce platform or institutional assurances (Ba and Pavlou 2002). Other institutional mechanisms such as third-party escrow services and credit card guarantees build trust in virtual marketplaces that extend throughout the community (Pavlou and Gefen 2004). Trust has been shown to be as important as perceived usefulness and perceived ease of use in the initial decision to engage in e-commerce (Gefen et al. 2003). In addition, longitudinal studies of trust in e-commerce have demonstrated that while its nature may change throughout the purchase process, it remains an important factor over time (Kim et al. 2009).

Trust also plays an important role in virtual teams. Trust development among members of a virtual team is a dynamic process and trust-building exercises can influence perceptions of ability, integrity, and benevolence which, in turn, influence trust among members (Jarvenpaa et al. 1998). Calculative, competence, and relational interpersonal trust are important antecedents of performance in of virtual

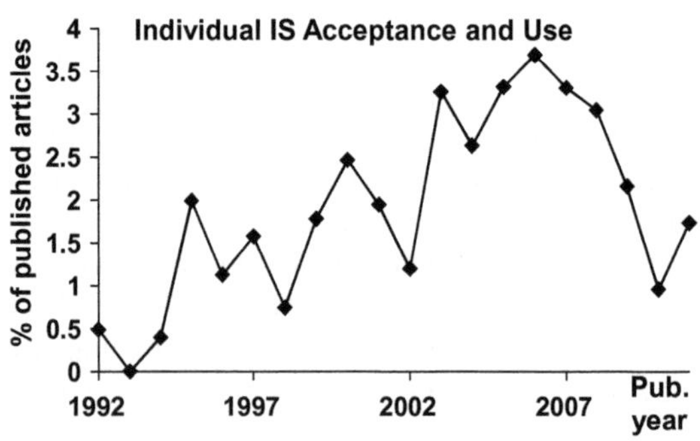

Fig. 5.2 Trends for individual IS acceptance and use

collaborative relationships (Paul and McDaniel 2004). If even one of these trust types is negative, it is highly likely to lead to reduced performance. The choice of controls is an important consideration in the development of trust among team members, and the use of traditional behavioral control mechanisms in the context of virtual teams has been shown to result in a significant negative effect on trust (Piccoli and Ives 2003).

Trust related IS research has experienced significant growth in the 2000s. Much of the growth in the 2000s can be assumed to be associated with e-commerce (Fig. 5.3).

Information Privacy: Ubiquitous computing and ubiquitous commerce that provides a high level of personalization promises to bring significant benefits. Technology that is location-aware can make suggestions based on user surroundings, e-commerce sites track purchases in order to make recommendations, and GPS-based tracking and alert systems integrated into automobiles can contact authorities in the event of an accident. However, this technology also raises personal privacy concerns and these concerns can act as a barrier to consumer adoption (Malhotra et al. 2004).

Information privacy is often used to refer to the desire of individuals to control their personal information (Bélanger and Crossler 2011). Issues that increase privacy concerns include: increased media attention given to the impacts of privacy issues (Henderson and Snyder 1999), news of security breaches, the increasing amount of data collected by government agencies and through government regulations (Henderson and Snyder 1999), and requiring information disclosure such as electronic health records (Angst and Agarwal 2009). While most would agree that absolute privacy is impossible, individuals must choose how to balance privacy concerns with perceived benefits (Dinev and Hart 2006).

For corporations, protecting personal information from improper use is both a responsibility and a challenge. Organizational policies and governmental regulations exist to guide corporate actions. In addition, one may argue that the organization has a moral obligation to safeguard consumer data and that responsibility should be engrained in the culture (Culnan and Clark Williams 2009).

Research in the area of information privacy is very diverse, ranging from development and validation of scales for measuring information privacy and

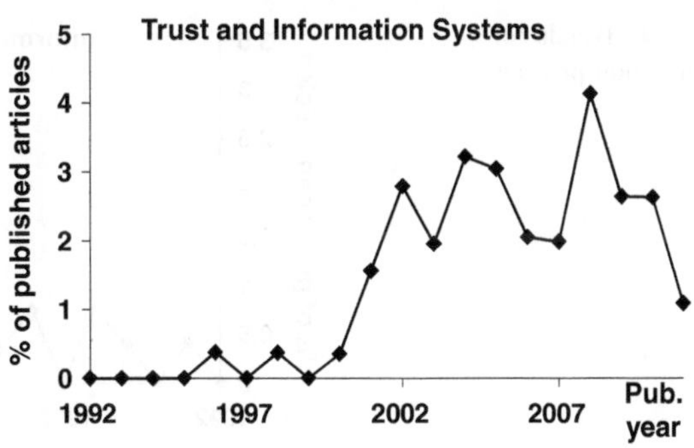

Fig. 5.3 Trends for trust and information systems

privacy practices (Smith et al. 1996) to the development of frameworks for the analysis of corporate privacy policies (Schwaig et al. 2006).

A major theme in the information privacy research is related to the tradeoffs between privacy risks and potential gains that drive consumer decision making. On the technology side, researchers have investigated the impact of different types of personalization systems and information delivery systems (i.e. push vs. pull) on decision making (Xu et al. 2010). Visibility of privacy statements can greatly reduce the perception of risk (Tsai et al. 2011), and privacy statements were found to have a greater impact on privacy risk perceptions than privacy seals (Hui et al. 2007). Financial incentives to entice consumers to share personal information have been found to greatly offset perceived privacy risk.

As technology has become more integrated into daily lives, concerns about privacy have increased. Not surprisingly, research in this area increased dramatically beginning in 2004. The trend has a strong upward trajectory (Fig. 5.4).

Learning and Training: The area of learning and training is broad and covers topic areas such as the effectiveness of self-guided and self-directed training, evaluation of e-learning systems and their impact on learning, the design of systems to enhance.

Today the need for individuals to learn more effectively and efficiently is greater than ever before. The level of skill and knowledge needed for most jobs is steadily increasing (Alavi 1994). In an attempt to address the growing challenges, work on technology assisted learning and training has increased as well.

Many of the technology assisted learning and training techniques require self-guided or self-regulated learning. The student must be disciplined and drive the pace of the learning process. Studies comparing self-guided and self-regulated learning have led to conflicting results. Professionals and managers preferred self-guided and self-regulated learning since it allowed them to take control of their own training (Gravill and Compeau 2008). However students needed to be incentivized or induced to follow self-regulated learning strategies. In the absence of the inducements, performance dropped off significantly (Santhanam et al. 2008).

In the evaluation of e-learning system effectiveness results have been inconsistent and appear to be context sensitive. Students in distance learning context were found to be more committed to their groups than students involved in

Fig. 5.4 Trends for information privacy

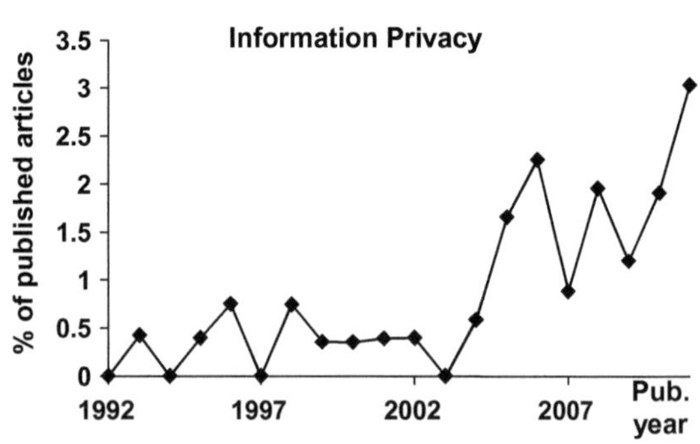

face-to-face instruction (Alavi et al. 1995) and differences in individual learning styles seem to have no significant impact on e-learning performance (Lu et al. 2003). The use of GDSS was found to lead to improved student performance, a higher level of perceived skill development, and improved perception of the class room experience (Alavi 1994). However, in the context of management training emails and listserv were more effective, compared to a sophisticated GSS system (Alavi et al. 2002). The use of a virtual learning environment was found to result in no difference in performance and left participants feeling less satisfied with the learning experience than a traditional classroom (Piccoli et al. 2001).

Several approaches to enhancing e-learning systems have been proposed. One such approach utilizes computer-supported collaborative learning lab that leverages immersive presence in an attempt to overcome some of the limitations of e-learning (Sharda et al. 2004). Another approach designed to overcome the lack of alignment between training and employee work performance involves highlighting the link between the training program, corporate goals and individual performance (Wang et al. 2011).

Research in the area of learning and training hit a peak in 1993 when it represented over 5 % of the articles published. After that, research in this area remained somewhat flat throughout 1990s and 2000s (Fig. 5.5).

5.2 Personal Computing Environments

End-User Computing: Proliferation of personal computers in the workplace and the use of computers by non-computer professionals resulted in increased research interest in end-user computing. End-user computing research spans areas such as computer usage, training, user support, the impact of computer usage, and economic issues. While early research focused on microcomputer usage, more recently interest has shifted to the newer technologies such as grid, network, and cloud computing.

Research on end-user training has yielded mixed findings. Training was found to have little or no impact on computer literacy (Winter et al. 1997). IS acceptance, IS

Fig. 5.5 Trends for learning and training

satisfaction and job satisfaction were found to be critical to successful end-user training (Lee et al. 1995). Playfulness was also found to positively influence training outcomes, mood, involvement and satisfaction regardless of the age of the trainee (Webster and Martocchio 1992). With respect to end-user support, the quality of documentation was found to be a strong factor in determining user satisfaction regardless of the user's level of experience (Torkzadeh and Doll 1993).

Computer usage in the workplace has been explored from multiple perspectives, including the effect of task uncertainty (Ghani 1992), task complexity (Mykytyn and Green 1992), and playfulness (Webster and Martocchio 1992) on computer usage. Quality and accessibility of information and the individual's personal style have been shown to influence the perceived usefulness of systems by managers (Kraemer et al. 1993).

More recent studies have focused on economic factors related to the adoption emerging technologies. Specifically, studies examined different pricing, economic and use-models models related to the adoption of grid and cloud computing (Zhang et al. 2008).

Research in the area of end-user computing peaked in the early 1990s and tapered off quickly. Very little work has been done in this area in recent years (Fig. 5.6).

Website Design: Research in the area of website design includes such diverse themes as website efficiency and successful traffic generation, client-centric design, the development of metrics for website design evaluation, and the effect of cultural orientation on website design and design effectiveness.

Website success is often measured by the site's ability to generate traffic. Studies show that factors such as download delay, content quality, interactivity, and responsiveness of the website can have a direct impact on website success (Palmer 2002). Website structure and page organization that facilitates information retrieval in an effective and efficient manner positively influences website success (Yen 2007). Capabilities that promote satisfaction and pleasure also contribute to website success (De et al. 2006).

Visit frequency to a particular website is heavily influenced by the level of trust on the part of the consumer. For less known websites, effective branding by the company can be effective in building trust among potential consumers (Lowry

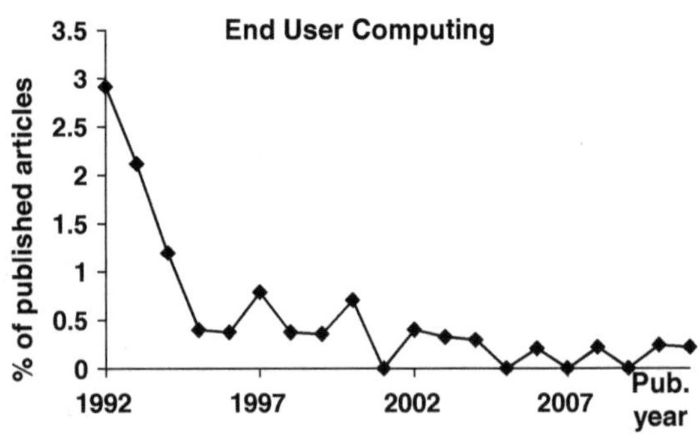

Fig. 5.6 Trends for end user computing

et al. 2008). In addition, overall satisfaction with the website (De Wulf et al. 2006) and website appeal (Hampton-Sosa and Koufaris 2005) contribute to trust building. Loyalty and commitment to the website can be established by building a relationship between the website and the consumer that goes beyond the typical business-to-consumer transactional relationship (Tomiuk and Pinsonneault 2009). As consumers become more loyal to a particular website, the stickiness (i.e., the amount of time users spend with a particular website) of that website is enhanced.

Several techniques have been used to measure website usability and website quality. Microsoft's Usability Guidelines (MUG), often with extensions, have been shown to be an accurate metric for website usability (Agarwal and Venkatesh 2002). WebQual 2.0 has also been shown to be an accurate metric for measuring website quality (Barnes and Vidgen 2001).

Cultural factors have been studied both from the perspective of their impact on website design and on consumer acceptance. Several studies examined the effect of cultural orientation with respect to communication context, individualism and power distance on web design (Usunier et al. 2009) and the ability of the website to convey subtle cultural messages through the use of animations and pictures (Zahedi and Bansal 2011).

Research on website design appeared in the mid 1990s, and exhibited a slightly upward trend throughout the 2000s, with a peak in 2002 (Fig. 5.7).

Mobile Computing: Mobile computing is characterized by the use of a computing platform which is designed to be portable. Mobile computing typically involves the use of a mobile device which employs an infrastructure or ad-hoc network in order to communicate with other computing resources. As devices continue to become smaller and more powerful, the impact of mobile computing on businesses and individuals is likely to increase. IS research on mobile computing has addressed general issues related to mobile computing as well as the application of mobile technologies in specific contexts. IS researchers have additionally designed prototypes to facilitate the use of mobile computing.

The expanded use of mobile computing calls for increased mobile work support. However, consistent with the task-technology fit model, perceived usefulness of mobile work support is influenced by task characteristics such as mobility, location dependency, and time criticality (Yuan et al. 2010). Adoption of mobile

Fig. 5.7 Trends for website design

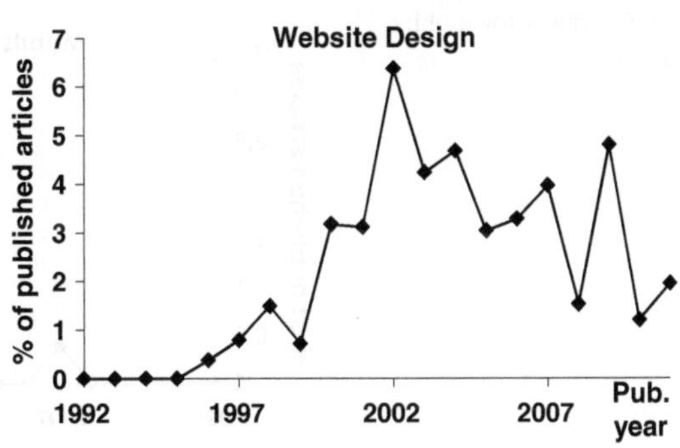

services has received considerable attention. Traditional TAM constructs (perceived ease of use and perceived usefulness) combined with elements of trust and resource characteristics influence the intention to use mobile services (Wang et al. 2006).

Mobile computing research is often context specific. A study of mobile banking services shows that relative benefits, propensity to trust and structural assurances influence trust, which is an important predictor of intention to use mobile banking services (Kim et al. 2009). In the mobile healthcare context, perceived service availability and personal innovativeness with IT, in combination with TAM constructs, predict adoption of mobile computing (Wu et al. 2011). In the transportation industry, organizations that employ sophisticated technologies in support of mobile ticketing are more likely to achieve higher performance gains than those that do not (Li et al. 2009). In the context of mobile commerce, security and adoption issues received significant attention (Juul and Jørgensen 2003; Lee et al. 2007).

IS research offers a number of technical solutions to facilitate mobile computing. Examples include pre-fetching and data caching strategy for mobile data warehousing (Huang and Lin 2005), a prototype middleware framework for transaction management in group-oriented mobile commerce (Varshney 2008), and the use of mobile agents for information retrieval in mobile data access systems (Jiao and Hurson 2004).

Mobile computing research emerged in the late 1990s, peaked in the 2000s, and stabilized in the 2010s (Fig. 5.8).

5.3 IT Effect on Careers and Jobs

IT and Jobs: High quality employees constitute one of the most important strategic resources for any company. As competitive pressures increase and technology moves forward, organizations must focus more attention on ways to maintain and enhance this strategic resource (Reich and Kaarst-Brown 1999). One of the key challenges facing organizations is how to attract and retain high quality information technology professionals.

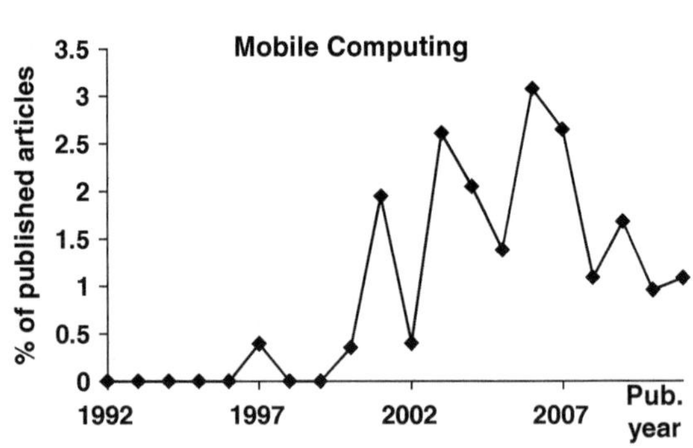

Fig. 5.8 Trends for mobile computing

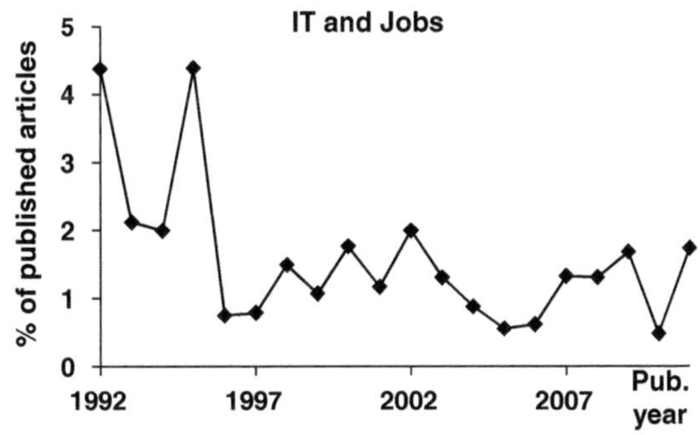

Fig. 5.9 Trends for IT and jobs

Retention of IT employees is one of the main research themes in the IT and jobs topic. Typical job stressors such as role ambiguity, role conflict and work exhaustion have been widely examined as drivers of job satisfaction organizational commitment, and turnover intentions (Allen et al. 2008; Guimaraes and Igbaria 1992).

Role ambiguity is one of the most influential drivers of job satisfaction but its effect is often moderated by attributes such as organizational tenure, age, and level of education (Igbaria and Guimaraes 1993). Emotional dissonance, the conflict between norms of displayed emotion and employee felt emotion (Rutner et al. 2008), and work overload (Moore 2000) have a negative impact on job satisfaction and increase in turnover intentions. High quality IT products positively impact job satisfaction (Joshi and Rai 2000) and reduce turnover intentions.

Research also examined issues related to career mobility and the transition from technical to non-technical roles (Reich and Kaarst-Brown 1999), performance differences between contract and full-time employees (Ang and Slaughter 2001), cyber-incivility (Lim and Teo 2009), and the impact of race (Igbaria and Wormley 1992) and gender (Igbaria and Baroudi 1995) on career advancement.

Research in the area of IT and jobs peaked in the early and mid-1990s. Throughout the late 1990s and 2000s, the research trend has been relatively flat with work accounting for between 0.5 and 2 % of the articles published (Fig. 5.9).

Fig. 5.9 Trends for IT and jobs

Chapter 6
IT and Markets

The Internet is the enabler of transactions between companies and individuals. Related research is generally focused on two broad research questions: (1) how does IT influence the markets (the macro level), and (2) how can trade be best conducted in the IT-enabled environment (the micro level). At the macro level, research includes such topics as on-line auctions and economics of IT and e-commerce. Much of this research is also related to the organizational use and consequences of IT. At the micro level, research examines marketing and customer relationship management issues in the context of e-commerce. The related topics include online consumer behavior, issues in e-commerce and customer service. These topics cover marketing issues, as well as issues related to the individual use of IT. The review of the research topics is presented in the following sections.

6.1 The Effect of IT on Markets

Issues in E-Commerce: E-commerce is the process by which goods or services are sold via electronic means and may entail business-to-business (B2B), business-to-consumer (B2C), or consumer-to-consumer (C2C) transactions. The late 1990s saw the emergence of viable e-commerce solutions, many of which were facilitated by various internet technologies, and the creation of electronic marketplaces. The emergence of e-commerce broadened the focus of IS research by extending the reach of organizational information systems outside of the boundaries of an enterprise (Straub and Watson 2001). Concomitant with the rise of e-commerce practice, IS researchers sought to examine issues pertinent to e-commerce including e-commerce success factors and e-commerce facilitating technologies.

The implementation success of e-commerce information systems has received considerable attention. The IS Success Model, as well as traditional IS success measures have been adapted and applied to e-commerce technologies and contexts (DeLone and McLean 2004) Research suggests that organizational constraints, the type of inter-organizational technology in use, as well as the external business

A. Sidorova et al., *A Survey of Core Research in Information Systems*,
SpringerBriefs in Computer Science, DOI: 10.1007/978-1-4614-7158-5_6,

environment influence the success of e-commerce efforts (Kaefer and Bendoly 2004; Poon 2000). Successful e-commerce initiatives require new enterprise architectures, and the development and implementation of such architectures requires significant organizational transformation (El Sawy et al. 1999).

Several studies have examined specific e-commerce enabling technologies. Examples include intelligent agents which can be trained to participate in e-commerce processes (Oliver 1997b), XML-based technologies (Van der Aalst and Kumar 2003), digital signatures (Gupta et al. 2004), and security assurances (Khazanchi and Sutton 2001) in the context of e-commerce. Such research is often concerned with improving or extending e-commerce capabilities in practice.

Finally, research efforts include the development of instruments for the measurement of e-commerce related constructs (Zhuang and Lederer 2003), assessments of the future implications of e-commerce practices (Zwass 1996), and analysis of the existing body of academic literature on the topic (Kauffman and Walden 2001). More recently, many of the same issues were examined in the context of mobile commerce (Ngai and Gunasekaran 2007).

Research on issues in e-commerce emerged in the early 1990s, peaked around 2000, and declined throughout the mid-to-late 2000s, possibly reflecting further specialization in ecommerce research (Fig. 6.1).

Economics of E-Commerce and IT: The proliferation of information technology and the access to the information provided by that technology has created a mechanism which fundamentally changes the way markets operate. Access to market and pricing information has increased dramatically for both buyers and sellers. The growing market transparency promised to alter the balance of power between buyers and sellers. As buyers are empowered to broaden their search for goods and services and rapidly compare prices, leverage may shift from the seller to the buyer (Oh and Lucas 2006).

In spite of the early predictions that ecommerce would drive prices down and intermediaries would effectively be squeezed out of the market, studies have shown that the actual situation is more complicated (Soh et al. 2006). Some studies suggest that products in buyer familiar markets have indeed experienced downward pricing pressure, while products in less familiar markets have either maintained their price level or actually increased in price (Clemons 2008). Factors

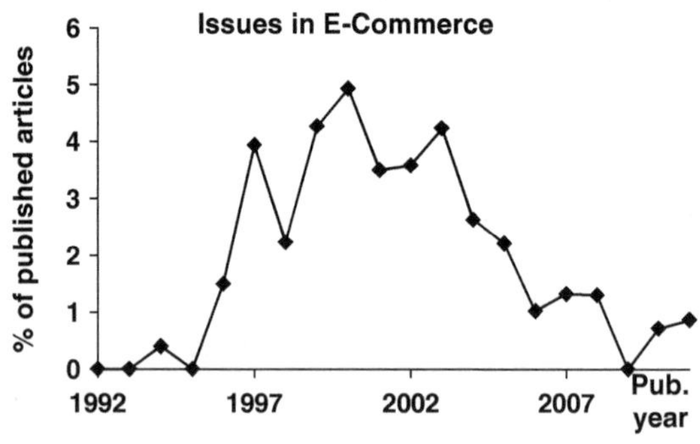

Fig. 6.1 Trends for issues in e-commerce

such as brand and vendor loyalty help maintain higher price levels (Kocas 2003). Uninformed buyers in online auctions have contributed to pushing prices higher for collectible items (Kauffman et al. 2009). Intentionally biasing information and distorting the market have emerged as issues in the electronic marketplace (Granados et al. 2010). Research results also point out to the evolution of the role of intermediaries in the ecommerce environment (Choudhury et al. 1998). Seller reputation and product condition have been considered in relation to pricing and time-to-sell (Ghose 2009), and new mechanisms for reducing product and seller-related uncertainty continue to be introduced.

Both fixed pricing and dynamic pricing models have been used in electronic marketplaces. With greater access to pricing and market data, sellers are better able to set and adjust prices based on changing market conditions. Within the context of fixed pricing, research focused on the frequency and magnitude of price adjustments, and the impact of such adjustments on consumer outrage and the perception of unfair pricing practices (Hinz et al. 2011). Dynamic pricing involves setting the price based on what the seller is willing to pay, and helps effectively avoid concerns over unfair pricing. Dynamic pricing strategies examined in IS research include threshold-based models, name your own price models (NYOP) (used by companies such as priceline.com), and online auctions (used by companies such as ebay.com) (Hinz et al. 2011, Kannan and Kopalle 2001).

In Business-to-Business (B2B) environments a variety of factors influence transactions in the electronic marketplace, including the number of suppliers and buyers within that market, the nature of the particular market, switching costs and buyer–seller relationships (Yoo et al. 2003).

Research in the area of the Economics of E-Commerce and IT trended steadily upward from 1992 until 2001, and the publication volume fluctuated widely throughout the 2000s (Fig. 6.2).

Online Auctions: The growth of the Internet and its associated technologies has resulted in the development of alternative methods of interactions for buyers and sellers. Online auctions represent a particularly successful mechanism for bringing buyers and sellers together in an electronic marketplace and provide a new avenue for Business-to-Business (B2B), Business-to-Consumer (B2C), and Consumer-to-Consumer (C2C) transactions. The success of companies such as eBay brought

Fig. 6.2 Trends for economics of e-commerce and IT

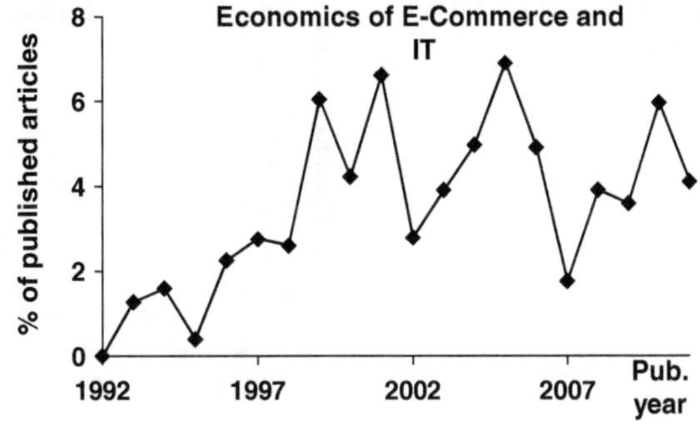

online auctions to the attention of a much wider audience. As consumer interest in online auctions grew, so did IS research regarding the phenomenon. Research related to online auctions is concentrated in three general areas: auction types, buyer-focused research, and seller-focused research.

There are a wide variety of auctions and significant research has been directed towards developing a deeper understanding of the implications of each auction type. A comparison of overlapping English auctions to uniform-price Dutch auctions found that the English auction format is superior in terms of revenue per unit (Bapna et al. 2009). A comparison of English versus Vickrey auctions determined that Vickrey second-price auctions offer advantages for modeling realistic price-demand functions (Barrot et al. 2010). This research stream also includes studies related to combinatorial auctions, such as a simulation study that benchmarks several iterative combinatorial auction formats (Bichler et al. 2009) and a comparison of linear versus non-linear price combinatorial auctions (Scheffel et al. 2011).

Buyer-focused research is largely focused on the bidding process and seeks to develop methods to maximize consumer surplus and improve the probability of winning. Bidders are a heterogeneous group, and they employ diverse bidding strategies (Bapna et al. 2004). The information available to consumers engaged in online auctions significantly impacts bidding strategy (Hinz and Spann 2008) and domain knowledge, rather than auction experience, leads to better adjustments for the "winner's curse" (Easley et al. 2011). Information systems such as DSS (Leskelä et al. 2007) and intelligent agents (Adomavicius et al. 2009) can be used to provide bidder support, thereby improving the odds of a bidder offering a winning bid.

The goal of seller-focused studies is optimization of the auction and maximizing revenue for the seller. The quality of a seller's e-image affects consumer's willingness to engage in commerce and increases prices received at auction (Gregg and Walczak 2008). Auction settings, including bid increment and ending rules also have an impact on bid price and revenue (Bapna et al. 2003; Onur and Tomak 2006).

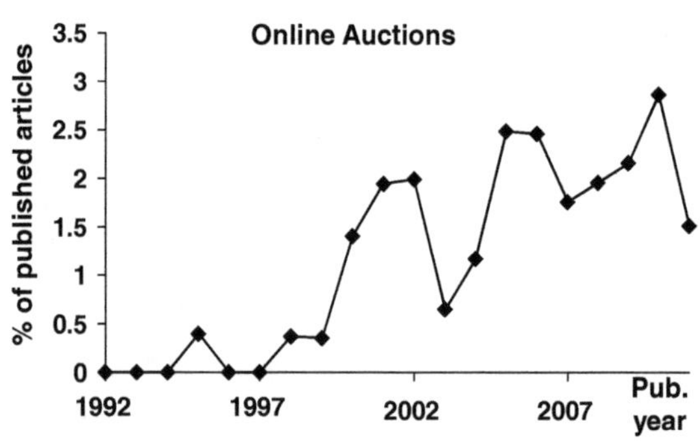

Fig. 6.3 Trends for online auctions

Online auction research emerged in the late 1990s as online auction web sites gained strength in the market. Despite sharp declines in 2003 and 2011, online auction research continues trending upward (Fig. 6.3).

6.2 Marketing and Consumer Behavior

Online Consumer Behavior: In the e-commerce environment, the consumer can be viewed as both a shopper and a computer user. Therefore, significant research efforts have been extended to better understanding the factors that influence consumer behavior with respect to e-commerce and online purchases. The richness of product presentation, the use of recommendation agents, and online reviews have been widely examined in relation to consumer intentions to return to a particular ecommerce site and online purchase decisions.

Richness of product presentation refers to the use of audio, pictures and virtual product presentations to enhance the consumer's online shopping experience. Research shows that vividness and interactivity of presentation positively influence the consumer's perceptions of diagnosticity, which leads to a more positive attitude toward the website; this positive attitude leads to an intention to purchase the product (Jiang and Benbasat 2007). The effectiveness of presentation richness can vary by personality traits: richness of presentation influences the buying behavior of intuitive and feeling types more than that of sensing and thinking types (Jahng et al. 2002).

The use of virtual reality (VR) can further enhance the presentation experience and influence buying behavior. VR enhances the consumers learning about a product when the important features of the product are made salient through visual and auditory cues. Furthermore, consumer learning is best enhanced when the products are highly experiential in nature (Suh and Lee 2005). Using VR to give the consumer visual control, the ability to manipulate product images, and functional control, the ability to explore functionality of the product, helps increase consumer's perceived diagnosticity (Jiang and Benbasat 2005).

Recommendation agents (RA's) are software agents that aid the consumer in making decisions by make suggestions based on the information gathered implicitly or explicitly about the consumer (Xiao and Benbasat 2007). The goal of recommendation agents is to reduce the impact of information overload; however, trust in the particular RA is a major concern. The consumer must trust that the RA has the competency to address their needs and that the RA is acting in the best interest of the consumer (Wang and Benbasat 2005).

Online reviews (OR's) facilitate informed buying decision-making by making the opinions of others available to the consumer. Online reviews tend to reduce consumer uncertainty and, therefore, increase market demand (Li et al. 2011). OR's helpfulness depends on the product type, the range of ratings, and depth of review (Mudambi and Schuff 2010), and the reviewer identity-descriptive information can increase the OR's impact on the consumer (Forman et al. 2008).

Fig. 6.4 Trends for online consumer behavior

Other themes in the online consumer behavior research include the use of infomediaries, websites that provide the consumer with product and pricing comparisons across a range of retailers (Son et al. 2006), the use of deceptive presentation techniques and deception detection approaches (Xiao and Benbasat 2011), security and privacy (Ranganathan and Ganapathy 2002), and trust (Gefen et al. 2003).

The volume of online consumer behavior research has been steadily increasing throughout late 1990s and 2000s (Fig. 6.4).

Customer Service: The relationship between buyer and seller in commercial transactions is crucial to the completion of the deal and to future commerce. Organizations invest in customer relationship by offering customer services before, during, and after a sale. Customer service activities take a variety of forms including helping the customer locate the best available product for their needs, recommending new products based on previous purchases, and the tracking of products during shipping. Information systems often enable customer service activities and research on customer services in the IS literature is prolific. Common themes include the customer services in the e-commerce context, customer service in systems development and support, and tools and methods for improving customer service.

The rise of electronic commerce has created customer service opportunities and challenges for organizations. Research has examined customer service in e-commerce in relation to customer satisfaction, customer loyalty, and trust. In e-commerce, a website represents the key interface between vendor and consumer. Web site quality, including information quality and system quality, is an important an antecedent of web-customer satisfaction, especially at the pre-purchase, information phase (McKinney et al. 2002). Post-purchase services such as support for order tracking, on-time delivery, and customer support are important factors in building customer loyalty (Otim and Grover 2006). Such convenience services are also of importance for creating customer satisfaction (Lee et al. 2003). Trust, another important component of the buyer–seller relationship, partially mediates the effect of service quality on customer loyalty (Gefen 2002).

A number of IT-based tools and methods have been examined in relation customer service. The use of web personalization techniques (e.g., user specific

Fig. 6.5 Trends for customer service

product recommendations) as a persuasion strategy has been found to yield positive results in the form of sales (Tam and Ho 2005). Wikis provide a self-service mechanism for influencing an organization's web presence, and can be used to develop customer engagement (Wagner and Majchrzak 2007). However, in the context of bricks-and-clicks organizations (companies with both a physical and web presence) self-service tools may undermine the ability of sales representatives to develop advisory relationships with customers (Schultze and Orlikowski 2004). IT tools, such as DSS, can also be used to determine if further investments in developing relationships with a given customer (such as the provision of various customer services) are justified given the anticipated economic benefits associated with the customer's purchases DSS (Chan and Ip 2011).

Customer service as related to systems support is another important research theme. Using a case study methodology, Shrednick et al. (1992) found that empowered, self-managed teams can substantially improve customer satisfaction in the context of information systems support. In the context of enterprise software system vendor support, both technical skills and behavioral skills of the support professional are found to be important determinants of customer satisfaction, although technical skills are more valued by repeat customers (Ramasubbu et al. 2008).

Customer service focused research is relatively sparse throughout the early to mid-1990s. However, customer service research volume grew in the late 1990s, and remained relatively stable throughout the 2000s. This is likely the result of the maturation of various Internet technologies and the emergence of e-commerce as an integral component of many organization's sales strategies (Fig. 6.5).

Fig. 6.5 Trends for customer service

Chapter 7
IT for Teamwork and Collaboration

From e-mails to mobile video-conferencing, Information systems play an important role in enabling communication among individuals. A significant amount of IS research is devoted to understanding the effect of the IT on communication and collaboration, including communication between individuals, teamwork, and the creation and development of larger virtual communities. This research can be can be broadly subdivided into two streams: the research on the broad effects of IT on communication and information sharing, and the research on how IT supports specific types of collaboration (groups, virtual teams, or virtual communities). Related topics are reviewed in the next sections.

7.1 IT for Communication and Information Sharing

Communication Media: In today's business environment managers and employees are confronted with a vast array of communication media that can be utilized to perform their day-to-day work activities (Watson-Manheim and Belanger 2007). Multi-national companies, geographically dispersed groups, and virtual teams make use of advanced communication media. Managers spend an estimated 85 % of their time communicating to peers, subordinates, customers, upper management, and other stakeholders (Adams et al. 1993). In the rapidly expanding world economy, it comes as no surprise that effective communication is viewed as strategically important by many companies (Adams et al. 1993). And understanding the effect of communication media on the communication process and outcomes is of paramount importance.

The media-richness theory (MRT) forms the theoretical grounding for communication media studies (Daft and Lengel 1984). Media richness theory characterizes communication media along a richness continuum from most rich (face-to-face) to least rich (numerical formal). The theory further posits that appropriate level of richness should be used to reduce uncertainty and minimize ambiguity in communications (Daft and Lengel 1984). However, studies using this

A. Sidorova et al., *A Survey of Core Research in Information Systems*, SpringerBriefs in Computer Science, DOI: 10.1007/978-1-4614-7158-5_7,

theory to evaluate the effectiveness of communication media have led to inconsistent finds. A study comparing face-to-face, electronic meetings, electronic conferencing and email found that richness did positively impact decision quality (Kahai and Cooper 2003). However, an investigation of team performance found no support for the impact of communication media richness on decision quality (Dennis and Kinney 1998).

As a result, alternative theoretical frameworks have been proposed. Critical social theory (CST) helps address the issue of contextualization in electronic communication (Ngwenyama and Lee 1997). Compensatory adaptation to communication media helps explain of some of the conflicting findings regarding MRT (Kock et al. 2006). Media synchronicity theory (MST) focuses on the ability of communication media to support communication goals, and suggests that there should be a fit between communication media and the type of communication process (Dennis et al. 2008).

Empirical research explored the comparative effects of different communication media on communication quality, effectiveness, and decision quality. Email was found to facilitate higher quality and more effective communication compared to instant messaging (Chen et al. 2008). Email was also found to have a greater impact to an organization than voicemail which was viewed more as a supplement to the telephone system (Adams et al. 1993). Group attributes such as group cohesion often have a greater impact on effective communication than the selection of a particular communication medium (Yoo and Alavi 2001). And the use of a variety of communication media can help enhance communication performance (Dennis et al. 2008).

The trend of research activity in the area of communication media has remained relatively steady over the past couple of decades. The number of articles published per year oscillates between less than 0.5 and 3.5 % (Fig. 7.1).

Knowledge Management: Knowledge is an important organizational resource that can be used for competitive advantage, and the objective of knowledge management and knowledge management systems (KMS) is to support the creation, transfer, and application of knowledge (Alavi and Leidner 2001; Sherif et al. 2006). Some of the major research streams in knowledge management include

Fig. 7.1 Trends for communication media

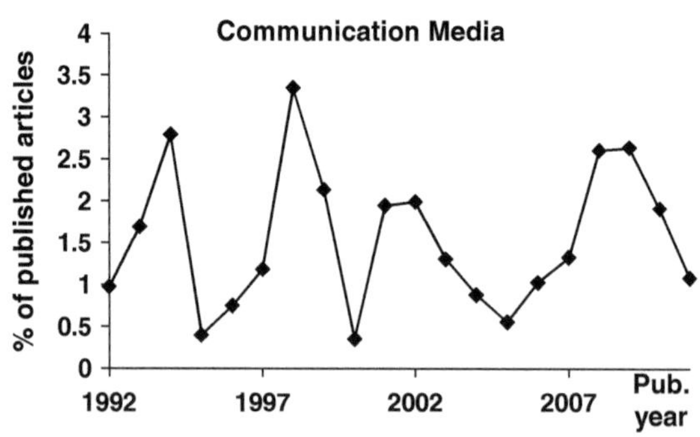

KMS implementation and use, knowledge sharing, knowledge seeking and use, and value to the firm.

Many KMS implementations failed due to the reluctance of employees to utilize the system. This has led many researchers to study factors that promote knowledge sharing. Studies have shown that self-efficacy, enjoyment in helping others (Kankanhalli et al. 2005), individual attitudes toward knowledge sharing, subjective norms, organizational climate (Bock et al. 2005), and reciprocity (Chang and Chuang 2011) influence individual willingness to share knowledge. The need for translation of individual knowledge, in conjunction with the individual tendency to hoard knowledge, negatively impacts knowledge sharing (Bock et al. 2005).

Knowledge seeking, use and reuse can take several forms, including expertise seeking by novices and secondary knowledge miners. Employees can seek to reuse their own knowledge at a later time or seek or reuse each other's knowledge (Markus 2001). Perceived usefulness, user satisfaction, organizational leadership and support (Kulkarni et al. 2007), and collaborative norms (Bock et al. 2006) have been shown to positively influence knowledge seeking and use. However, contrary to expectations, employee incentives have been inconsistent in their influence on knowledge seeking (Bock et al. 2005; Kankanhalli et al. 2005).

Determining whether or not KMS enhance the performance of the firm has proven difficult and has often led to inconsistent findings (Sherif et al. 2006). Research suggests that KMS implementations that succeed in creating synergies between cross-functional groups within an organization positively impact overall firm performance (Tanriverdi 2005). However, a poorly implemented KMS can lead to negative results for the organization (Shin 2004). Culture, both at the national and organizational level influences knowledge sharing and issues related to system design and implementation (Trice and Davis 1993). The degree to which organizational behavior and culture is conducive to knowledge sharing is strong factor in KMS success (Wang et al. 2008). Fit between the KMS implementation and knowledge task in question influences both performance and utilization (Teo and Men 2008).

Research in the area of knowledge management has been relatively steady throughout the 2000s, accounting for 2–4 % of published articles (Fig. 7.2).

Fig. 7.2 Trends for knowledge management

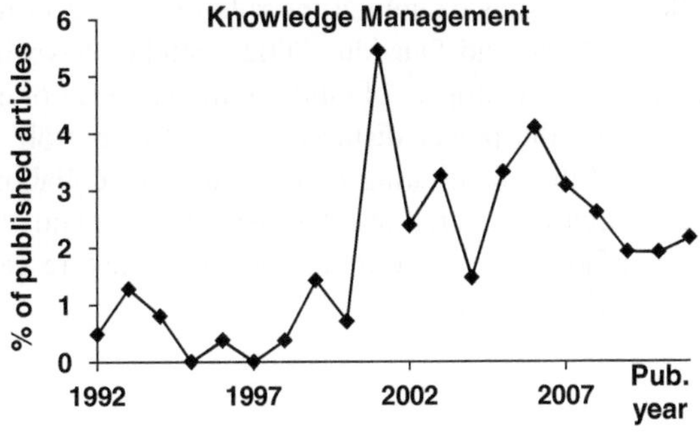

7.2 IT-Supported Team-Work and Virtual Communities

Group Support Systems (GSS): GSS are a collection of technologies, software, and processes that are designed to facilitate and enhance group work activities (e.g., communication, cooperation, deliberations, decision making, etc.) (Dennis et al. 1997). GSS research streams have included the impact of GSS on the organization and GSS effectiveness, application domains, system design and cultural influences.

GSS performance within an organization is influenced by many factors including: the specific task, the nature of the group, and level of support and facilitation (Dennis and Wixom 2002; Zigurs and Buckland 1998). The fit-appropriation model of GSS use suggests that GSS performance is impacted by two factors: the fit between the task and the GSS structure, and the level of support the group receives to help incorporate the system into work activities (Dennis et al. 2001). Although GSS systems have been shown to improve information exchange among group members, the impact on effective decision making is sometimes lacking (Dennis 1996).

At a more granular level, studies have shown that GSS influence group dynamics by leveling out individual influence within the workgroup (Huang and Wei 1997). GSS can have a positive influence on task-related interactions, while at the same time dampening social interactions (Huang and Wei 2000). Effective GSS implementations and facilitation can have a positive impact on individual knowledge acquisition (Kwok et al. 2003). As with any system, GSS can also be misused to advance individual agendas and facilitate deception within the group (George et al. 2008).

Design of GSS and supporting processes have been show to influence GSS effectiveness. Group facilitators have been shown to have a positive impact on group productivity. Facilitators often focus on areas such as individual group member anxiety, system use and reliability (Niederman et al. 1996), and coordination (Nan and Johnston 2009). The incorporation of mechanisms that regulate the flow of information in order to reduce information overload is shown to aid in information processing (Grisé and Gallupe 2000). GSS have been used in many different application areas including: strategic planning (Dennis et al. 1997) and conflict management (Miranda and Bostrom 1994).

Several studies examined the role of culture in relation to GSS use and effectiveness (Tung and Quaddus 2002). Studies have indicated that the use of GSS may dampen the impact of cultural differences. For example, GSS can be effective in reducing the power distance effects by controlling communication within the group and thus facilitating more productive collaboration (Tan et al. 1995).

Research in the area of GSS peaked in the late 1990s. Subsequently interest in the area faded. Since the mid-2000s, little new research has been published in the area of GSS (Fig. 7.3).

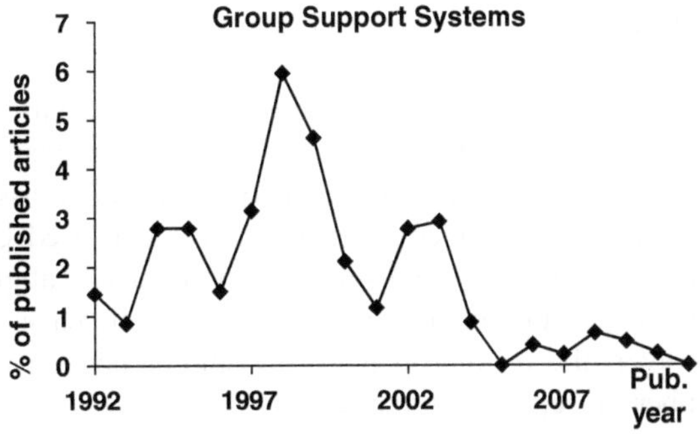

Fig. 7.3 Trends for group support systems

Virtual Teams: A virtual team is a group of individuals which operate across temporal, spatial, or organizational boundaries in order to achieve a common goal. Such teams are often assembled on an "as-needed" basis and disbanded or reassigned at the conclusion of a project. In recent years, organizations have taken advantage of virtual teams in order to better utilize organizational resources, exploit individual expertise, and diversify team composition. Information and Communication Technology (ICT) has played a key role in the rise of virtual teaming arrangements by providing support for team communication, organization, and control. IS research on virtual teams has grown concomitantly with the increase in their use by organizations. The vast majority of IS research has been directed at understanding factors that lead to virtual team effectiveness, such as team trust, use of technology, and leadership.

A number of studies examine the relationship between the use of virtual teams within organizations (commonly referred to as "virtuality" or "virtualness") and organizational effectiveness and/or performance (Chudoba et al. 2005; Schweitzer and Duxbury 2010). Increasing virtuality is often found to be associated with decreased effectiveness (Schweitzer and Duxbury 2010), which underscores the importance of more fully understanding how organizations can improve virtual team effectiveness.

Several frameworks for understanding the antecedents of virtual team effectiveness have been proposed (Furst et al. 1999). Trust among virtual team members has been shown to play a critical role. The concept of trust within virtual teams has been shown to be complex and situationally dependent (Jarvenpaa et al. 2004). Individual perceptions of other team members significantly influence trust and the importance of these perceptions varies over time (Jarvenpaa et al. 1998). While trust-building exercises and training can be used effectively to build trust (Warkentin and Beranek 1999), control mechanisms associated with traditional teams may decrease trust (Piccoli and Ives 2003).

Effective leadership is critical to virtual team success. Characteristics of effective virtual team leaders include willingness to mentor, empathy for team members, ability to assert authority without being perceived as overbearing, and ability to provide effective communication (Kayworth and Leidner 2002). Effective leaders value personal relationships with virtual team members (Pauleen

2004) and play the role of coordinator in order to reduce team conflict (Wakefield et al. 2008).

Collaboration technologies are often used by virtual teams and may be adapted to better accommodate the needs of the team (Majchrzak et al. 2000). Collaboration and communication technologies are often associated with improved team outcomes. For instance, virtual teams which used GSS were found to be more democratic and produced solutions more closely aligned with the interest of team members as opposed to those dictated by team leaders (Dennis and Garfield 2003). However, the uncontrolled use of communication technologies may result in a number of negative outcomes such as communication bottlenecks (Sengupta and Zhao 1998), and disruption of organizational knowledge transfer processes (Griffith et al. 2003).

Following the growing organizational reliance on virtual teams, IS research related to virtual teams has increased throughout the late 1990 and 2000s. This trend is likely to continue in the near future as organizations leverage collaboration and communications technologies to make more efficient use of their human resources (Fig. 7.4).

Virtual Worlds and Virtual Communities: The evolution of Internet technologies combined with improved graphics and processing power of personal computers have enabled the development of immersive computer simulated environments. These virtual worlds allow users, who are typically represented by an avatar, to interact with one another and with objects in the world. Examples of these immersive 3-D environments range from virtual worlds with social and commercial goals (e.g., SecondLife) to worlds in which entertainment and gaming goals are featured (e.g., World of Warcraft).

Virtual worlds have received considerable interest in recent years. Several factors have been shown to drive individual engagement with virtual worlds and ensure virtual worlds remain viable. Research suggests that individuals continue using virtual worlds based on their perceptions of usefulness, enjoyment, and automatic behaviors (Barnes 2011). Cognitive absorption and conceptualizing the virtual world as a "place" also contribute to user continuous use and user engagement (Goel et al. 2011). Potential applications for virtual world technologies include areas which require a high degree of coordination and

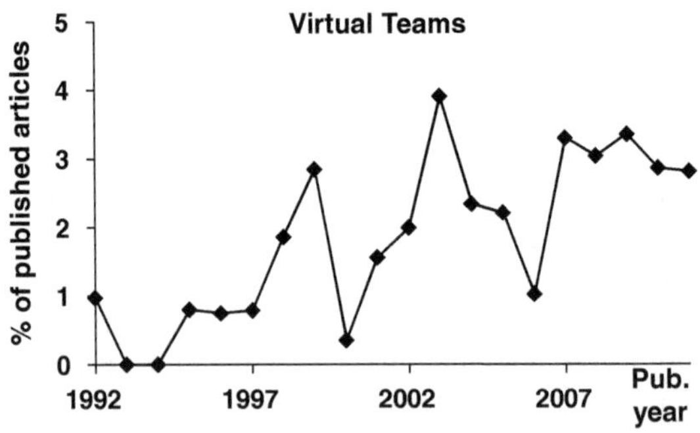

Fig. 7.4 Trends for virtual teams

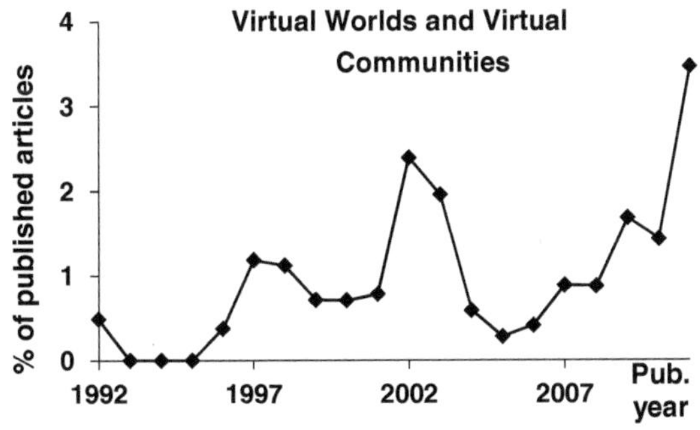

Fig. 7.5 Trends for virtual worlds and virtual communities

communication. Examples include collaboration (Davis et al. 2009), knowledge management (Mueller et al. 2011), and education (Eschenbrenner et al. 2008).

Virtual worlds have been used as settings for studying economic behavior of individuals, such as purchasing behaviors for both virtual and real world goods. For instance a model of virtual purchasing behavior identifies intrinsic and extrinsic motivations that predict intentions to purchase virtual goods (Guo and Barnes 2011). Virtual world environments can facilitate buying of real goods. The use of avatars that closely resemble the user has been shown to improve the user's ability to evaluate the quality and performance of apparel (Suh et al. 2011), suggesting applications in shopping situations in which the user is required to envision using a product.

Related but distinct from the virtual worlds research, is research on virtual communities. Virtual communities are collectivities of individual (often geographically dispersed) who share common interests or pursue common goals, and rely on electronic media for communication and coordination of activities. Virtual communities may or may not be formed in the context of a virtual world. Research studies typically focus on the formation and use of virtual communities. Formation of a successful virtual community is a complex process and may be impacted by both virtual and real world factors. Inhibitors to the creation of a virtual community have been classified into technological, motivational, task, or system-related (Wilde and Swatman 1997). The sense of virtual community is impacted by the enthusiasm of community leaders, off-line activities available to community members, and enjoyability associated with the use of the community (Koh and Kim 2003). And the impact of these factors is stronger for communities that originated online versus those that originated offline and migrated to a virtual environment.

IS research on virtual worlds is relatively scarce, with significant volume fluctuations. In late 2000s, the topic exhibited a strong upward trend. While this research topic accounts for just over 1 % of published articles over that time period, in 2011 this research stream accounted for over 3.5 % of published articles, perhaps, partially due to a special issue of MIS Quarterly entitled "New Ventures in Virtual Worlds" (Fig. 7.5).

Chapter 8
Conclusion

In this book we describe the more prominent topics of IS research and relate them to the five broad IS research areas: IT artifact and IS development, IT and organizations, IT and individuals, IT and markets and IT for teamwork and collaboration.[1] Within each of the research areas, the topics are organized into sub-areas. We present an organizing framework for IS research.

The presented framework highlights the coherent, albeit diverse structure of the IS research. In spite of the numerous concerns about the missing IT artifact, the IT artifact is strongly present not only in the IS design and development research, but also in research on classes of organizational IS, as well as personal computing environment.

The framework also highlights how the IS discipline seeks to balance the rigor versus relevance needs of the applied discipline. Within each broad research area, researchers seek to address the long-term theoretical issues, as well as incorporate the technological and organizational trends. For example, within IT artifact and IS development research area, research addresses the fundamental issues of IS design and modeling, but also seeks to apply such design principles to specific types of IS. As technology and management fashions change, the research moves from decision support systems, to expert systems, to business analytics.

Similarly, in the area of IT and organizations, researchers seek to uncover the more general factors influencing organizational IS use and management, but also try to make their research more relevant by looking at how these factors apply to specific classes of organizational IS. As organizations moved from EDI to SCM, so shifts the context of organizational IS research. At the individual level, the need for rigor and relevance is achieved by examining factors that influence IS adoption and use, and then applying the findings to the changing personal computing environments, from end-user computing, to web-based computing to mobile computing.

---

[1] It is also important to note that due to the space considerations and the imposition of the 51-topic limit, the list of IS topics is not exhaustive. For example, such topics as business process management and soft systems methodologies did not emerge among the top 51 topics, and thus were not included in the description. This does not mean that such topics are not relevant or important to IS research.

A. Sidorova et al., *A Survey of Core Research in Information Systems*,
SpringerBriefs in Computer Science, DOI: 10.1007/978-1-4614-7158-5_8,

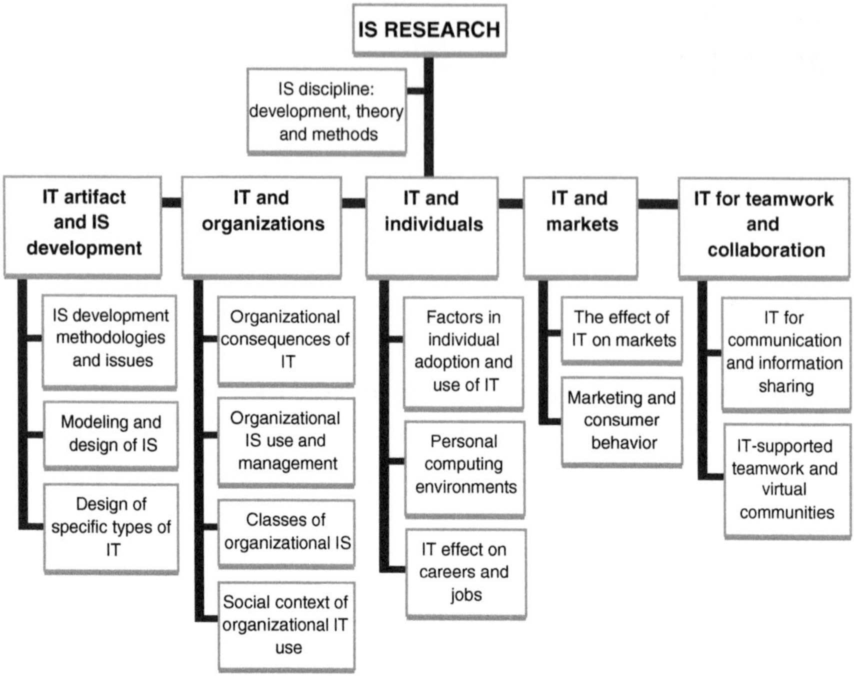

Fig. 8.1 An organizing framework of IS research

We hope by organizing and reviewing the main areas of IS research, we give IS researchers an opportunity to view the IS discipline as a whole, and to get a better understanding on how the individual pieces of the IS research puzzle fit together. This will, hopefully, make IS researchers more confident about the value and progress of the IS discipline, and will help them better communicate this value to their students and industry practitioners (Fig. 8.1).

Appendix
Bibliometric Study of the IS Body of Research

Reviewing an academic discipline is closely related to defining its intellectual structure. A variety of approaches have been used to define the intellectual structure of the IS academic discipline, including qualitative literature analysis, manual coding according to a pre-defined classification scheme (Vessey et al. 2002), co-citation analysis (Culnan 1987; Taylor et al. 2010), and latent semantic analysis (Sidorova et al. 2008). In this book we use the latent semantic analysis approach to identify key research areas and topics in IS literature, as we consider it the most appropriate method for capturing and organizing the highly conceptual semantic content in the body of published IS research. It is also an approach that avoids, to a large extent, interpretive bias, and offers a reasonable level of computational efficiency.

About LSA

Latent Semantic Analysis (LSA) was introduced in the late 1980s as a method for indexing free-text documents (Deerwester et al. 1990). Early approaches to document indexing were based on the Vector Space Model (VSM). The VSM represents documents as vectors in a multi-dimensional space where each dictionary term is a dimension. In matrix form, the VSM of a collection of documents (a *corpus*) is a matrix where the rows are the dictionary terms and the columns are the documents in the collection. The matrix entries are frequency counts, indicating how many times a particular term appears in a particular document. Using the VSM, document similarities are computed as dot products of the corresponding vectors (columns in the term frequency matrix). Such a computation of similarity which focuses on the words that are literally present in the documents has two main shortcomings. The first refers to the fact that VSM considers all words out of their context. For example, a query about "legal rights" may return documents that talk about directions as in "first turn left, then turn right." This is known as the *polysemy* problem. The second shortcoming refers to the fact that VSM fails to capture similarity between words that are different but

A. Sidorova et al., *A Survey of Core Research in Information Systems*,
SpringerBriefs in Computer Science, DOI: 10.1007/978-1-4614-7158-5,

conceptually similar, such as synonyms and metaphors. This is known as the *synonymy* problem. To address these shortcomings, LSA introduced a matrix operation that decomposes the term frequency matrix into term eigenvectors, document eigenvectors, and square roots of eigenvalues (*singular values*). The decomposition is called Singular Value Decomposition (SVD) and is closely related to principal component analysis. SVD represents terms and documents in a space of ordered latent semantic dimensions which correspond to components of variability in the VSM. Keeping all the available dimensions allows us to recreate the original term frequency matrix. However, keeping only the first k dimensions reproduces a truncated version of the term frequency matrix, which ignores low-level patterns that describe language usage and focuses on high-level patterns that describe concepts. Researchers in psychology, cognitive science, and linguistics, have found that the high-level dimensions can help explain a number of cognitive functions, including the learning and understanding of word meaning, semantic memory, discourse coherence, and the comprehension of metaphors. The factor analysis variant of LSA focuses on the high-level dimensions that describe socially constructed concepts. Outcomes of factor-analytic LSA include high-loading terms and high-loading documents for each factor. High-loading terms show how the document authors articulate the concepts. High-loading documents show how the concepts are manifested in the document collection. Top-loading documents provide best examples of documents that describe the concepts. Our bibliometric study follows factor-analytic LSA and applies it to a collection of published article abstracts, as introduced in Sidorova et al. (2008). The following sections provide details on our data collection, analysis, and results.

Data Collection

IS article data were collected using the electronic library Business Source Complete, housed at EBSCO Host. In order to capture a relatively mature stage in the development of the IS discipline, we limited the scope of our coverage to the 1992–2011 period. However, articles published in the 1985–1991 period were *folded in*[1] to our extracted factors and are also included in our topic reviews. We focused on contributing research articles, therefore editorials, commentaries, news stories, announcements, and book reviews, were excluded. A careful manual verification of the data downloaded from EBSCO revealed a number of errors, including missing articles and incomplete abstracts, which were corrected. Table A.1 lists the 10 journals included in our bibliometric study with the final article count. A total of 6,518 articles were included in our data set. For eight of these journals we have complete coverage of their published articles in the 1992–2011 period, since they were already in print in 1992. The remaining two

[1] This means that while the topics were identified based on the 1992–2011 literature, we also consider earlier publications related to the extracted topics.

Table A.1 Collected IS articles

Journal name (in alphabetical order)	Coverage	Article count
Decision Support Systems	1992–2011	1,753
European Journal of Information Systems	1992–2011	603
Information and Management	1992–2011	1,108
International Journal of E-Commerce	1996–2011	342
Information Systems Journal	1992–2011	349
Information Systems Research	1992–2011	489
Journal of the AIS	2000–2011	260
Journal of Database Management	1992–2011	331
Journal of MIS	1992–2011	726
MIS Quarterly	1992–2011	557
Total	1992–2011	6,518

journals have reduced coverage due to unavailability: *International Journal of Electronic Commerce* was established in 1996 and *Journal of the Association for Information Systems* was established in 2000. Our main analysis focused on the article abstracts, as they represent concise and carefully crafted representations of each article's intellectual contribution.

Analysis

Our analysis extends the analysis of 1,615 article abstracts performed in Sidorova et al. (2008). Here we provide a high-level discussion of our analysis. We refer readers who are interested in the methodological details to the online Appendices A and C of Sidorova et al. (2008). In our analysis we also followed the recommendations in Evangelopoulos et al. (2012). Our analysis was performed using custom-made Java code that replicates the LSA implementation in SAS® Enterprise Miner 6.1 or newer, with text mining module Text Miner 4.2 or newer. LSA can also be performed using an open-access LSA package that is available in the R software environment, after some minor coding adjustments, as well as the open source text mining package Rapidminer 5.2.

As a pre-processing step, since our analysis is based on the abstracts' language, we converted words that appeared in British English spelling to American English spelling. This was the case with a sizeable subset of abstracts appearing in the *European Journal of Information Systems* and *Information Systems Journal*. Following best practices in text mining, we filtered out trivial, high-frequency English words such as *and*, *of*, *the*, etc. Terms that appeared only once in the entire collection were also filtered out, as they cannot participate in the formation of any patterns in term usage. The remaining terms were stemmed. For example, *service*, *services*, *serviced*, and *servicing*, were all replaced by *servic-*. The resulting vocabulary consisted of 6,099 non-trivial stemmed terms that appeared in the set of 6,518 abstracts at least twice. Following the communality filtering approach described in Sidorova et al. (2008), these terms were ranked based on their ability to explain variance among the top 100 principal components obtained through a first round of Singular Value Decomposition. The top 20 terms, ordered by descending communality, were: *Information_Technologi-*, *Information_System-*, *knowledge-*, *model-*, *decision-*, *project-*, *DSS*, *user-*, *trust-*, *team-*, *servic-*, *system-*, *inform-*, *softwar-*, *price-*, *network-*, *market-*, *web-*, *outsourc-*, and *firm-*. These 20 stemmed terms explained a combined total of 25% of variability produced by the first 100 principal components. Indeed, one could easily compile an extended definition of "IS research" using these 20 terms! Extending the list of terms to the top 753 allowed us to explain 95% of variability. Referring to Kuhn (1996, pp. 136–138), these 753 terms are the basic vocabulary of scientific language in IS research, not from the perspective of the authors of the present book at the time of its writing, but from the perspective of the original IS research article contributors, at the time of *their* writing. The rest of the analysis was based on these 753 stemmed terms.

The collection of 6,518 abstracts was quantified following the Vector Space Model approach, as a 753-by-6,518 matrix were the frequency of occurrence of each one of the 753 terms in each one of the 6,518 documents was recorded. Following best practices in text mining, the occurrence of high-frequency terms was discounted and the occurrence of low-frequency terms was promoted using the Inverse Document Frequency (TF-IDF) transformation. The resulting matrix was subjected to Singular Value Decomposition. After retaining the top 51 factors, the factor space was rotated to produce a simplified term loading structure using the varimax rotation procedure. In a similar manner, the five factor solution was produced.

Results

Factor labeling involved the examination of high loading terms and documents. The labels were selected to reflect the nature of research associated with each factor. The five factors in the five-factor solution corresponded well to the factors in Sidorova et al. (2008), and were labeled as follows: F5.1—*IT artifact and IS development*, F5.2—*IT and organizations*, F5.3—*IT and individuals*, F5.4—*IT and markets*, and F5.5—*IT for teamwork and collaboration*. The labels for the 51 factor solution are shown in Table A.2, together with counts of high-loading articles for each factor. The produced five-factor and fifty-one-factor solutions correspond to the research areas and the research topics in the IS, respectively. The correspondence between the specific areas and the topics was examined using the counts of cross-loading documents for each research-area-topic pair.

Table A.2 Extracted topics in IS research

Factor	Label	Article count
F01	IS Theories, Frameworks, and Methods	855
F02	IS Success Factors	381
F03	Economics of E-Commerce and IT	244
F04	Business Analytics/Data Mining	207
F05	Online Consumer Behavior	208
F06	Algorithms and Problem Solving	171
F07	Website Design	157
F08	Data Management and Database Design	167
F09	Decision Support Systems	130
F10	Virtual Teams	132
F11	IT Investments and Firm Value	129
F12	Online Auctions	89
F13	Instrument Development and Validation	129
F14	Individual IS Acceptance and Use	135
F15	Decision Modeling	75
F16	IT Capabilities and Firm Performance	94
F17	Modeling Techniques and Approaches	113
F18	Diffusion of Innovation	135
F19	Enterprise Resource Planning Systems	85
F20	Electronic Data Interchange	81
F21	Software Development and Use	138
F22	Outsourcing and Labor Sourcing	101
F23	Group Support Systems	97
F24	Strategic Information Systems Planning	111
F25	Intelligent Agents	133
F26	Trust and Information Systems	107
F27	Supply Chain Management	99
F28	Issues in E-Commerce	119
F29	IS Security	100
F30	Control	39
F31	IS Discipline	102
F32	Networks	119
F33	Knowledge Management	133
F34	IS Risk Management	96
F35	Communication Media	101
F36	Customer Service	106
F37	Learning and Training	108
F38	Expert Systems	104
F39	IT and Jobs	95
F40	Cultural Issues in IS	76
F41	Information Search and Retrieval	104
F42	Mobile Computing	76
F43	Object Oriented Approaches	81
F44	Systems Development Methodologies	87
F45	Information Privacy	69

(continued)

Table A.2 (continued)

Factor	Label	Article count
F46	E-Government	64
F47	Executive Information Systems	67
F48	Virtual Worlds and Virtual Communities	68
F49	End User Computing	29
F50	Rule-Based Systems	40
F51	Error Detection and Management	31

References

Adams D, Todd P, Nelson R (1993) A comparative evaluation of the impact of electronic and voice mail on organizational communication. I&M 24(1):9–21

Adomavicius G, Gupta A, Zhdanov D (2009) Designing intelligent software agents for auctions with limited information feedback. ISR 20(4):507–526

Agarwal R, Karahanna E (2000) Time flies when you're having fun: cognitive absorption and beliefs about information technology usage. MISQ 24(4):665–694

Agarwal R, Venkatesh V (2002) Assessing a firm's web presence: a heuristic evaluation procedure for the measurement of usability. ISR 13(2):168–186

Agarwal R, Sinha A, Tanniru M (1996) Cognitive fit in requirements modeling: a study of object and process methodologies. JMIS 13(2):137–162

Alavi M (1994) Computer-mediated collaborative learning: an empirical evaluation. MISQ 18(2):159–174

Alavi M, Carlson P (1992) A review of MIS research and disciplinary development. JMIS 8(4):45–62

Alavi M, Kayworth T, Leidner D (2006) An empirical examination of the influence of organizational culture on knowledge management practices. JMIS 22(3):191–224

Alavi M, Leidner D (2001) Review: knowledge management and knowledge management systems: conceptual foundations and research issues. MISQ 25(1):107–136

Alavi M, Marakas G, Yoo Y (2002) A comparative study of distributed learning environments on learning outcomes. ISR 13(4):404–415

Alavi M, Wheeler B, Valacich J (1995) Using IT to reengineer business education: an exploratory investigation of collaborative telelearning. MISQ 19(3):293–312

Alfaro E, García N, Gámez M, Elizondo D (2008) Bankruptcy forecasting: an empirical comparison of AdaBoost and neural networks. DSS 45(1):110–122

Allen M, Armstrong D, Reid M, Riemenschneider C (2008) Factors impacting the perceived organizational support of IT employees. I&M 45(8):556–563

Anderson C, Agarwal R (2010) Practicing safe computing: a multi method empirical examination of home computer user security behavioral intentions. MISQ 34(3):613–A15

Ang S, Slaughter S (2001) Work outcomes and job design for contract versus permanent information systems professionals on software development teams. MISQ 25(3):321–350

Ang S, Straub D (1998) Production and transaction economies and IS outsourcing: a study of the U.S. banking industry. MISQ 22(4):535–552

Angeles R, Nath R (2000) An empirical study of EDI trading partner selection criteria in customer-supplier relationships. I&M 37(5):241–255

Angst C, Agarwal R (2009) Adoption of electronic health records in the presence of privacy concerns: the elaboration likelihood model and individual persuasion. MISQ 33(2):339–370

A. Sidorova et al., *A Survey of Core Research in Information Systems*,
SpringerBriefs in Computer Science, DOI: 10.1007/978-1-4614-7158-5,

Asvanund A, Clay K, Krishnan R, Smith M (2004) An empirical analysis of network externalities in peer-to-peer music-sharing networks. ISR 15(2):155–174
Ba S, Pavlou P (2002) Evidence of the effect of trust building technology in electronic markets: price premiums and buyer behavior. MISQ 26(3):243–268
Bakos J, Nault B (1997) Ownership and investment in electronic networks. ISR 8(4):321–341
Balaban M, Shoval P (1999) Enhancing the ER model with integrity methods. JDM 10(4):14–23
Baldwin L, Irani Z, Love P (2001) Outsourcing information systems: drawing lessons from a banking case study. EJIS 10(1):15–24
Banker R, Slaughter S (2000) The moderating effects of structure on volatility and complexity in software enhancement. ISR 11(3):219–240
Banville C, Landry M (1989) Can the field of MIS be disciplined? Commun ACM 32(1):48–60
Bapna R, Chang S, Goes P, Gupta A (2009) Overlapping online auctions: empirical characterization of bidder strategies and auction prices. MISQ 33(4):763–783
Bapna R, Goes P, Gupta A (2003) Replicating online Yankee auctions to analyze auctioneers' and bidders' strategies. ISR 14(3):244–268
Bapna R, Goes P, Gupta A, Jin Y (2004) User heterogeneity and its impact on electronic auction market design: an empirical exploration. MISQ 28(1):21–43
Barfod M, Salling K, Leleur S (2011) Composite decision support by combining cost-benefit and multi-criteria decision analysis. DSS 51(1):167–175
Barkhi R, Rolland E, Butler J, Fan W (2005) Decision support system induced guidance for model formulation and solution. DSS 40(2):269–281
Barki H, Rivard S, Talbot J (2001) An integrative contingency model of software project risk management. JMIS 17(4):37–69
Barnes S (2011) Understanding use continuance in virtual worlds: empirical test of a research model. I&M 48(8):313–319
Barnes S, Vidgen R (2001) An evaluation of cyber-bookshops: the WebQual method. IJEC 6(1):11
Barrot C, Albers S, Skiera B, Schäfers B (2010) Vickrey vs. eBay: why second-price sealed-bid auctions lead to more realistic price-demand functions. IJEC 14(4):7–38
Barthélemy J, Geyer D (2005) An empirical investigation of IT outsourcing versus quasi-outsourcing in France and Germany. I&M 42(4):533–542
Barua A, Lee B (1997) An economic analysis of the introduction of an electronic data interchange system. ISR 8(4):398–422
Baskerville R (1993) Semantic database prototypes. ISJ 3(2):119–144
Baskerville R, Pries-Heje J (1998) Information technology diffusion: building positive barriers. EJIS 7(1):17–28
Basu A, Blanning R (1994) Model integration using metagraphs. ISR 5(3):195–218
Beath C, Orlikowski W (1994) The contradictory structure of systems development methodologies: deconstructing the IS-user relationship in information engineering. ISR 5(4):350–377
Beeri Y, Spiegler I (1996) Synergetic expert systems. DSS 17(2):73–82
Bélanger F, Crossler R (2011) Privacy in the digital age: a review of information privacy research in information systems. MISQ 35(4):1017–A36
Benaroch M, Lichtenstein Y, Robinson K (2006) Real options in information technology risk management: an empirical validation of risk-option relationships. MISQ 30(4):827–864
Benbasat I, Barki H (2007) Quo vadis, TAM? JAIS 8(4):212–218
Benbasat I, Weber R (1996) Research commentary: rethinking "diversity" in information systems research. ISR 7(4):389–399
Benbasat I, Zmud R (1999) Empirical research in information systems: the practice of relevance. MISQ 23(1):3–16
Benbasat I, Zmud R (2003) The identity crisis within the IS discipline: defining and communicating the discipline's core properties. MISQ 27(2):183–194
Bera P, Krasnoperova A, Wand Y (2010) Using ontology languages for conceptual modeling. JDM 21(1):1

Bergeron F, Raymond L, Rivard S, Gara M (1995) Determinants of EIS use: testing a behavioral model. DSS 14(2):131–146

Bharadwaj A (2000) A resource-based perspective on information technology capability and firm performance: an empirical investigation. MISQ 24(1):169–196

Bhatt G, Grover V (2005) Types of information technology capabilities and their role in competitive advantage: an empirical study. JMIS 22(2):253–277

Bhattacherjee A (2002) Individual trust in online firms: scale development and initial test. JMIS 19(1):211–241

Bichler M, Shabalin P, Pikovsky A (2009) A computational analysis of linear price iterative combinatorial auction formats. ISR 20(1):33–59

Bidgoli H (2004) The internet encyclopedia 1, vol 1. Wiley, Hoboken

Bock G, Kankanhalli A, Sharma S (2006) Are norms enough? the role of collaborative norms in promoting organizational knowledge seeking. EJIS 15(4):357–367

Bock G, Zmud R, Kim Y, Lee J (2005) Behavioral intention formation in knowledge sharing: examining the roles of extrinsic motivators, social-psychological forces, and organizational climate. MISQ 29(1):87–111

Boley D, Gini M, Gross R, Han E, Hastings K, Karypis G, Kumar V, Mobasher B, Moore J (1999) Partitioning-based clustering for web document categorization. DSS 27(3):329–341

Booch G (2000) Unifying enterprise development teams with the UML. JDM 11(4):37–39

Bose I, Mahapatra R (2001) Business data mining: a machine learning perspective. I&M 39(3):211–225

Boss S, Kirsch L, Angermeier I, Shingler R, Boss R (2009) If someone is watching, I'll do what I'm asked: mandatoriness, control, and information security. EJIS 18(2):151–164

Boudreau M, Gefen D, Straub D (2001) Validation in information systems research: a state-of-the-art assessment. MISQ 25(1):1–16

Bradley J (1992) An object-relationship diagrammatic technique for object-oriented database definitions. JDM 3(2):1–11

Bryson N, Ngwenyama O (2000) Structuring IS outsourcing contracts for mutual gain: an approach to analyzing performance incentive schemes. JAIS 1:9

Bui T, Lee J (1999) An agent-based framework for building decision support systems. DSS 25(3):225–237

Burton-Jones A, Meso P (2006) Conceptualizing systems for understanding: an empirical test of decomposition principles in object-oriented analysis. ISR 17(1):38–60

Butler B (2001) Membership size, communication activity, and sustainability: a resource-based model of online social structures. ISR 12(4):346–362

Carter L, Bélanger F (2005) The utilization of e-government services: citizen trust, innovation and acceptance factors. ISJ 15(1):5–25

Castner G, Ferguson C (2000) The effect of transaction costs on the decision to replace "off-the-shelf" software: the role of software diffusion and infusion. ISJ 10(1):65–83

Cerpa N, Verner J (1998) Case study: the effect of IS maturity on information systems strategic planning. I&M 34(4):199–208

Chai S, Kim M, Rao H (2011) Firms' information security investment decisions: stock market evidence of investors' behavior. DSS 50(4):651–661

Chan S, Ip W (2011) A dynamic decision support system to predict the value of customer for new product development. DSS 52(1):178–188

Chander P, Shinghal R, Radhakrishnan T (1997) Using goals to design and verify rule bases. DSS 21(4):281–305

Chang H, Chuang S (2011) Social capital and individual motivations on knowledge sharing: participant involvement as a moderator. I&M 48(1):9–18

Chang Lee K, Kwon S (2008) A cognitive map-driven avatar design recommendation DSS and its empirical validity. DSS 45(3):461–472

Chatterjee D, Pacini C, Sambamurthy V (2002) The shareholder-wealth and trading-volume effects of information-technology infrastructure investments. JMIS 19(2):7–42

Chatzoglou P (1997) Use of methodologies: an empirical analysis of their impact on the economics of the development process. EJIS 6(4):256–270

Chau M, Chen H (2008) A machine learning approach to web page filtering using content and structure analysis. DSS 44(2):482–494

Chen A, Goes P, Marsden J (2003) A query-driven approach to the design and management of flexible database systems. JMIS 19(3):121–154

Chen K, Yen D, Hung S, Huang A (2008) An exploratory study of the selection of communication media: the relationship between flow and communication outcomes. DSS 45(4):822–832

Chen M (1995) A model-driven approach to accessing managerial information: the development of a repository-based executive information system. JMIS 11(4):33–63

Chen W, Hirschheim R (2004) A paradigmatic and methodological examination of information systems research from 1991 to 2001. ISJ 14(3):197–235

Cheung W, Babin G (2006) A meta database-enabled executive information system (part A): a flexible and adaptable architecture. DSS 42(3):1589–1598

Chi R, Turban E (1995) Distributed intelligent executive information systems. DSS 14(2):117–130

Chiravuri A, Nazareth D, Ramamurthy K (2011) Cognitive conflict and consensus generation in virtual teams during knowledge capture: comparative effectiveness of techniques. JMIS 28(1):311–350

Choi D (2003) Enhancing the power of web search engines by means of fuzzy query. DSS 35(1):31–44

Choudhury V, Sabherwal R (2003) Portfolios of control in outsourced software development projects. ISR 14(3):291–314

Choudhury V, Hartzel K, Konsynski B (1998) Uses and consequences of electronic markets: an empirical investigation in the aircraft parts industry. MISQ 22(4):471–507

Chua C, Cao L, Cousins K, Straub D (2003) Measuring researcher-production in information systems. JAIS 3:145–215

Chudoba K, Wynn E, Lu M, Watson-Manheim M (2005) How virtual are we? Measuring virtuality and understanding its impact in a global organization. ISJ 15(4):279–306

Chwelos P, Benbasat I, Dexter A (2001) Research report: empirical test of an EDI adoption model. ISR 12(3):304–321

Clark T, Jones M, Armstrong C (2007) The dynamic structure of management support systems: theory development, research focus, and direction. MISQ 31(3):579–615

Clemons E, Row M (1991) Sustaining IT advantage: the role of structural differences. MISQ 15(3):275–292

Comes T, Hiete M, Wijngaards N, Schultmann F (2011) Decision maps: a framework for multi-criteria decision support under severe uncertainty. DSS 52(1):108–118

Compeau D, Higgins C (1995) Computer self-efficacy: development of a measure and initial test. MISQ 19(2):189–211

Contreras I (2011) Emphasizing the rank positions in a distance-based aggregation procedure. DSS 51(1):240–245

Cremonini M, Nizovtsev D (2010) Risks and benefits of signaling information system characteristics to strategic attackers. JMIS 26(3):241–274

Culnan M (1987) Mapping the intellectual structure of MIS, 1980–1985: A Co-citation analysis. MISQ 11(3):341–353

Culnan M, Clark Williams C (2009) How ethics can enhance organizational privacy: lessons from the choice point and TJX data breaches. MISQ 33(4):673–687

D'arcy J, Hovav A, Galletta D (2009) User awareness of security countermeasures and its impact on information systems misuse: a deterrence approach. ISR 20(1):79–98

Daft R, Lengel R (1984) Information richness: a new approach to managerial behavior and organization design. Res Organ Behav 6:191–234

Darmont J, Schneider M (2000) Benchmarking OODBs with a generic tool. JDM 11(3):16–27

Davenport T, Markus M (1999) Rigor vs. relevance revisited: response to Benbasat and Zmud. MISQ 23(1):19–23

Davis A, Murphy J, Owens D, Khazanchi D, Zigurs I (2009) Avatars, people, and virtual worlds: foundations for research in metaverses. JAIS 10(2):90–117

Davis F (1986) A technology acceptance model for empirically testing new end-user information systems: theory and results. Doctoral Dissertation, Massachusetts Institute of Technology, Cambridge

Davis F (1989) Perceived usefulness, perceived ease of use, and user acceptance of information technology. MISQ 13(3):319–340

Dawande M, Johar M, Kumar S, Mookerjee V (2008) A comparison of pair versus solo programming under different objectives: an analytical approach. ISR 19(1):71–92

De Wulf K, Schillewaert N, Muylle S, Rangarajan D (2006) The role of pleasure in web site success. I&M 43(4):434–446

Dean D, Lowry P, Humpherys S (2011) Profiling the research productivity of tenured information systems faculty at U.S. Institutions. MISQ 35(1):1–15; A1–A8

Deerwester S, Dumais S, Furnas G, Landauer T, Harshmans R (1990) Indexing by latent semantic analysis. J Am Soc Inf Sci 41(6):391–407

DeLone W, McLean E (1992) Information systems success: the quest for the dependent variable. ISR 3(1):60–95

DeLone W, McLean E (2003) The DeLone and McLean model of information systems success: a ten-year update. JMIS 19(4):9–30

DeLone W, McLean E (2004) Measuring e-commerce success: applying the DeLone and McLean information systems success model. IJEC 9(1):31–47

Deng P, Fuhr C (1995) Using an object-oriented approach to the development of a relational database application system. I&M 29(2):107–121

Dennis A (1996) Information exchange and use in group decision making: you can lead a group to information, but you can't make it think. MISQ 20(4):433–457

Dennis A, Garfield M (2003) The adoption and use of GSS in project teams: toward more participative processes and outcomes. MISQ 27(2):289–323

Dennis A, Kinney S (1998) Testing media richness theory in the new media: the effects of cues, feedback, and task equivocality. ISR 9(3):256–274

Dennis A, Wixom B (2002) Investigating the moderators of the group support systems use with meta-analysis. JMIS 18(3):235–257

Dennis A, Fuller R, Valacich J (2008) Media, tasks, and communication processes: a theory of media synchronicity. MISQ 32(3):575–600

Dennis A, Tyran C, Vogel D, Nunamaker J Jr (1997) group support systems for strategic planning. JMIS 14(1):155–184

Dennis A, Valacich J, Fuller M, Schneider C (2006) Research standards for promotion and tenure in information systems. MISQ 30(1):1–12

Dennis A, Wixom B, Vandenberg R (2001) Understanding fit and appropriation effects in group support systems via meta-analysis. MISQ 25(2):167–193

Dinev T, Hart P (2006) An extended privacy calculus model for e-commerce transactions. ISR 17(1):61–80

Doll W, Raghunathan T, Lim J, Gupta Y (1995) A confirmatory factor analysis of the user information satisfaction instrument. ISR 6(2):177–188

Dos Santos B, Peffers K, Mauer D (1993) The impact of information technology investment announcements on the market value of the firm. ISR 4(1):1–23

Downing C, Ringuest J (2002) Implementing and testing a complex interactive MOLP algorithm. DSS 33(4):363–374

Draft R, Lengel R (1984) Information richness: a new approach to managerial behavior and organization design. Res Organ Behav 6:191–234

Du S, Keil M, Mathiassen L, Shen Y, Tiwana A (2007) Attention-shaping tools, expertise, and perceived control in IT project risk assessment. DSS 43(1):269–283

Easley R, Wood C, Barkataki S (2011) Bidding patterns, experience, and avoiding the winner's curse in online auctions. JMIS 27(3):241–268
Ein-Dor P, Spiegler I (1995) Natural language access to multiple databases: a model and a prototype. JMIS 12(1):171–197
El Sawy O, Malhotra A, Gosain S, Young K (1999) IT-intensive value innovation in the electronic economy: insights from Marshall industries. MISQ 23(3):305–335
Eom S, Lee S, Kim J (1993) The intellectual structure of decision support systems (1971–1989). DSS 10(1):19–35
Eschenbrenner B, Nah F, Siau K (2008) 3-D virtual worlds in education: applications, benefits, issues, and opportunities. JDM 19(4):91–110
Evangelopoulos N, Zhang X, Prybutok V (2012) Latent semantic analysis: five methodological recommendations. EJIS 21(1):70–86
Evermann J (2005) Towards a cognitive foundation for knowledge representation. ISJ 15(2):147–178
Evermann J, Wand Y (2009) Ontology based object-oriented domain modeling: representing behavior. JDM 20(1):48–77
Fan W, Gordon M, Pathak P (2005) Genetic programming-based discovery of ranking functions for effective web search. JMIS 21(4):37–56
Fan W, Gordon M, Pathak P (2006) On linear mixture of expert approaches to information retrieval. DSS 42(2):975–987
Fazlollahi B, Vahidov R (2001) A method for generation of alternatives by decision support systems. JMIS 18(2):229–250
Fazlollahi B, Parikh M, Verma S (1997) Adaptive decision support systems. DSS 20(4):297–315
Fishbein M, Ajzen I (1975) Belief, attitude, intention, and behavior: an introduction to theory and research. Addison-Wesley, Reading
Fitzgerald B (1997) The use of systems development methodologies in practice: a field study. ISJ 7(3):201–212
Fitzgerald B (1998) An empirical investigation into the adoption of systems development methodologies. I&M 34(6):317–328
Fitzgerald B (2006) The transformation of open source software. MISQ 30(3):587–598
Flynn D, Hepburn P (1994) Strategic planning for information systems: a case study of a United Kingdom metropolitan council. EJIS 3(3):207–217
Fonseca F, Martin J (2007) Learning the differences between ontologies and conceptual schemas through ontology-driven information systems. JAIS 8(2):129–142
Forman C, Ghose A, Wiesenfeld B (2008) Examining the relationship between reviews and sales: the role of reviewer identity disclosure in electronic markets. ISR 19(3):291–313
Francalanci C, Galal H (1998) Information technology and worker composition: determinants of productivity in the life insurance industry. MISQ 22(2):227–241
Furst S, Blackburn R, Rosen B (1999) Virtual team effectiveness: a proposed research agenda. ISJ 9(4):249–269
Galletta D, Hartzel K, Johnson S, Joseph J, Rustagi S (1997) Spreadsheet presentation and error detection: an experimental study. JMIS 13(3):45–63
Galliers R (2003) Change as crisis or growth? Toward a trans-disciplinary view of information systems as a field of study: a response to Benbasat and Zmud's call for returning to the IT artifact. JAIS 4(6):337–351
Gallivan M, Benbunan-Fich R (2007) Analyzing IS research productivity: an inclusive approach to global IS scholarship. EJIS 16(1):36–53
Gallivan M, Depledge G (2003) Trust, control and the role of interorganizational systems in electronic partnerships. ISJ 13(2):159–190
Gattiker T, Goodhue D (2005) What happens after ERP implementation: understanding the impact of inter-dependence and differentiation on plant-level outcomes. MISQ 29(3):559–585
Geerts P, Vermeir D, Nute D (1994) Ordered logic: defeasible reasoning for multiple agents. DSS 11(2):157–190

Gefen D (2002) Customer loyalty in e-commerce. JAIS 3:27–51
Gefen D, Straub D (2000) The relative importance of perceived ease of use in IS adoption: a study of e-commerce adoption. JAIS 1:8
Gefen D, Karahanna E, Straub D (2003) Trust and TAM in online shopping: an integrated model. MISQ 27(1):51–90
George J, Marett K, Giordano G (2008) Deception: toward an individualistic view of group support systems. JAIS 9(10):653–676
Ghani J (1992) Task uncertainty and the use of computer technology. I&M 22(2):69–76
Ghose A (2009) Internet exchanges for used goods: an empirical analysis of trade patterns and adverse selection. MISQ 33(2):263–291
Gill T (1995) Early expert systems: where are they now? MISQ 19(1):51–81
Gill G, Bhattacherjee A (2009) Whom are we informing? Issues and recommendations for MIS research from an informing sciences perspective. MISQ 33(2):217–235
Goel L, Johnson N, Junglas I, Ives B (2011) From space to place: predicting users' intentions to return to virtual worlds. MISQ 35(3):749–A5
Goode S (2005) Something for nothing: management rejection of open source software in Australia's top firms. I&M 42(5):669–681
Goodhue D, Thompson R (1995) Task-technology fit and individual performance. MISQ 19(2):213–236
Gordon L, Loeb M, Sohail T (2010) Market value of voluntary disclosures concerning information security. MISQ 34(3):567–A2
Gosain S, Malhotra A, El Sawy O (2005) Coordinating for flexibility in e-business supply chains. JMIS 21(3):7–45
Goswami S, Chan H, Kim H (2008) The role of visualization tools in spreadsheet error correction from a cognitive fit perspective. JAIS 9(6):321–343
Granados N, Gupta A, Kauffman R (2006) The impact of IT on market information and transparency: a unified theoretical framework. JAIS 7(3):148–177
Gravill J, Compeau D (2008) Self-regulated learning strategies and software training. I&M 45(5):288–296
Gregg D, Walczak S (2008) Dressing your online auction business for success: an experiment comparing two eBay businesses. MISQ 32(3):653–670
Gregor S (2006) The nature of theory in information systems. MISQ 30(3):611–642
Gregor S, Jones D (2007) The anatomy of a design theory. JAIS 8(5):312–335
Griffith T, Sawyer J, Neale M (2003) Virtualness and knowledge in teams: managing the love triangle of organizations, individuals, and information technology. MISQ 27(2):265–287
Grisé M, Gallupe R (2000) Information overload: addressing the productivity paradox in face-to-face electronic meetings. JMIS 16(3):157–185
Grover V, Goslar M (1993) The initiation, adoption, and implementation of telecommunications technologies in U.S. organizations. JMIS 10 (1):141-163
Grover V, Segars A (2005) An empirical evaluation of stages of strategic information systems planning: patterns of process design and effectiveness. I&M 42(5):761–779
Grover V, Ayyagari R, Gokhale R, Lim J (2006) about reference disciplines and reference differences: a critique of Wade et al. JAIS 7(5):336–349
Guimaraes T, Igbaria M (1992) Determinants of turnover intentions: comparing IC and IS personnel. ISR 3(3):273–303
Guo K, Yuan Y, Archer N, Connelly C (2011) Understanding nonmalicious security violations in the workplace: a composite behavior model. JMIS 28(2):203–236
Guo Y, Barnes S (2011) Purchase behavior in virtual worlds: an empirical investigation in second life. I&M 48(7):303–312
Gupta A, Tung Y, Marsden J (2004) Digital signature: use and modification to achieve success in next generational e-business processes. I&M 41(5):561–575
Gupta M, Rees J, Chaturvedi A, Chi J (2006) Matching information security vulnerabilities to organizational security profiles: a genetic algorithm approach. DSS 41(3):592–603

Hadar I, Soffer P (2006) Variations in conceptual modeling: classification and ontological analysis. JAIS 7(8):568–592
Hall J, Liedtka S (2005) Financial performance, CEO compensation, and large-scale information technology outsourcing decisions. JMIS 22(1):193–221
Hammer P, Kogan A (1996) Essential and redundant rules in Horn knowledge bases. DSS 16(2):119–130
Hampton-Sosa W, Koufaris M (2005) The effect of web site perceptions on initial trust in the owner company. IJEC 10(1):55–81
Han H, Lee J, Seo Y (2008) Analyzing the impact of a firm's capability on outsourcing success: a process perspective. I&M 45(1):31–42
Harvey L (1997) A genealogical exploration of gendered genres in IT cultures. ISJ 7(2):153–172
Henderson S, Snyder C (1999) Personal information privacy: implications for MIS managers. I&M 36(4):213–220
Henggeler Antunes C, Almeida L, Lopes V, Clímaco J (1994) A decision support system dedicated to discrete multiple criteria problems. DSS 12(4–5):327–335
Henry R, McCray G, Purvis R, Roberts T (2007) Exploiting organizational knowledge in developing IS project cost and schedule estimates: an empirical study. I&M 44(6):598–612
Herath T, Rao H (2009) Encouraging information security behaviors in organizations: role of penalties, pressures and perceived effectiveness. DSS 47(2):154–165
Hevner A, March S, Park J, Ram S (2004) Design science in information systems research. MISQ 28(1):75–105
Higa K (1996) An approach to improving the maintainability of existing rule bases. DSS 18(1):23–31
Hinz O, Spann M (2008) The impact of information diffusion on bidding behavior in secret reserve price auctions. ISR 19(3):351–368
Hinz O, Hann I, Spann M (2011) Price discrimination in e-commerce? An examination of dynamic pricing in name-your-own price markets. MISQ 35(1):81–A10
Hirschheim R, Kleinim H (1994) Realizing emancipatory principles in information systems development: the case for ETHICS. MISQ 18(1):83–109
Hitt L, Wu D, Zhou X (2002) Investment in enterprise resource planning: business impact and productivity measures. JMIS 19(1):71–98
Hofstede G (1980) Culture's consequences: international differences in work-related values. Sage, Beverly Hills
Hofstede G (1991) Cultures and organizations. McGraw-Hill, London
Huang S, Lin B (2005) Intelligent cache management for mobile data warehouse systems. JDM 16(2):46–65
Huang W, Wei K (1997) Task as a moderator for the effects of group support systems on group influence processes. EJIS 6(4):208–217
Huang W, Wei K (2000) An empirical investigation of the effects of group support systems (gss) and task type on group interactions from an influence perspective. JMIS 17(2):181–206
Huang Z, Chen H, Hsu C, Chen W, Wu S (2004) Credit rating analysis with support vector machines and neural networks: a market comparative study. DSS 37(4):543–558
Hui K, Teo H, Lee S (2007) The value of privacy assurance: an exploratory field experiment. MISQ 31(1):19–33
Huisman M, Iivari J (2006) Deployment of systems development methodologies: perceptual congruence between IS managers and systems developers. I&M 43(1):29–49
Iacovou C, Benbasat I, Dexter A (1995) Electronic data interchange and small organizations: adoption and impact of technology. MISQ 19(4):465–485
Igbaria M, Baroudi J (1995) The impact of job performance evaluations on career advancement prospects: an examination of gender differences in the IS workplace. MISQ 19(1):107–123
Igbaria M, Guimaraes T (1993) Antecedents and consequences of job satisfaction among information center employees. JMIS 9(4):145–174

Igbaria M, Wormley W (1992) Organizational experiences and career success of MIS professionals and managers: an examination of race differences. MISQ 16(4):507–529
Iivari J, Huisman M (2007) The relationship between organizational culture and the deployment of systems development methodologies. MISQ 31(1):35–58
Iivari J, Hirschheim R, Klein H (1998) A paradigmatic analysis contrasting information systems development approaches and methodologies. ISR 9(2):164–193
Irani Z, Love P, Elliman T, Jones S, Themistocleous M (2005) Evaluating e-government: learning from the experiences of two United Kingdom local authorities. ISJ 15(1):61–82
Jahng J, Jain H, Ramamurthy K (2002) Personality traits and effectiveness of presentation of product information in e-business systems. EJIS 11(3):181–195
Janvrin D, Morrison J (2000) Using a structured design approach to reduce risks in end user spreadsheet development. I&M 37(1):1–12
Jarupathirun S, Zahedi F (2007) Dialectic decision support systems: system design and empirical evaluation. DSS 43(4):1553–1570
Jarvenpaa S, Knoll K, Leidner D (1998) Is anybody out there? JMIS 14(4):29–64
Jarvenpaa S, Shaw T, Staples D (2004) Toward contextualized theories of trust: the role of trust in global virtual teams. ISR 15(3):250–264
Jeyaraj A, Rottman J, Lacity M (2006) A review of the predictors, linkages, and biases in IT innovation adoption research. J Inf Technol 21(1):1–23
Ji Y, Mookerjee V, Sethi S (2005) Optimal software development: a control theoretic approach. ISR 16(3):292–306
Jiang J, Klein G, Carr C (2002) Measuring information system service quality: SERVQUAL from the other side. MISQ 26(2):145–166
Jiang Z, Benbasat I (2005) Virtual product experience: effects of visual and functional control of products on perceived diagnosticity and flow in electronic shopping. JMIS 21(3):111–147
Jiang Z, Benbasat I (2007) Investigating the influence of the functional mechanisms of online product presentations. ISR 18(4):454–470
Jiao Y, Hurson A (2004) Application of mobile agents in mobile data access systems: a prototype. JDM 15(4):1–24
Johnston A, Warkentin M (2010) Fear appeals and information security behaviors: an empirical study. MISQ 34(3):549–A4
Jones C, Hilton T, Lutz C (1998) Discovering objects: which identification and refinement strategies do analysts really use? JDM 9(3):3–14
Joosten S, Purao S (2002) A rigorous approach for mapping workflows to object-oriented IS models. JDM 13(4):1–19
Joshi K, Rai A (2000) Impact of the quality of information products on information system users' job satisfaction: an empirical investigation. ISJ 10(4):323–345
Jung-Ho A, Kim H (2002) The Soprano extensible object storage system. JDM 13(1):15–24
Juul N, Jørgensen N (2003) The security hole in WAP: an analysis of the network and business rationales underlying a failure. IJEC 7(4):73–92
Kaefer F, Bendoly E (2004) Measuring the impact of organizational constraints on the success of business-to-business e-commerce efforts: a transactional focus. I&M 41(5):529–541
Kahai S, Cooper R (2003) Exploring the core concepts of media richness theory: the impact of cue multiplicity and feedback immediacy on decision quality. JMIS 20(1):263–299
Kankanhalli A, Tan B, Wei K (2005) Contributing knowledge to electronic knowledge repositories: an empirical investigation. MISQ 29(1):113–143
Kannan P, Kopalle P (2001) Dynamic pricing on the internet: importance and implications for consumer behavior. IJEC 5(3):63–83
Karimi J, Somers T, Bhattacherjee A (2007) The impact of ERP implementation on business process outcomes: a factor-based study. JMIS 24(1):101–134
Kartseva V, Hulstijn J, Gordijn J, Tan Y (2010) Control patterns in a health-care network. EJIS 19(3):320–343

Kasap N, Aytug H, Erenguc S (2007) Provider selection and task allocation issues in networks with different QoS levels and all you can send pricing. DSS 43(2):375–389

Kasper G (1996) A theory of decision support system design for user calibration. ISR 7(2):215–232

Kauffman R, Walden E (2001) Economics and electronic commerce: survey and directions for research. IJEC 5(4):5–116

Kauffman R, McAndrews J, Wang Y (2000) Opening the 'Black Box' of network externalities in network adoption. ISR 11(1):61–82

Kauffman R, Spaulding T, Wood C (2009) Are online auction markets efficient? An empirical study of market liquidity and abnormal returns. DSS 48(1):3–13

Kayande U, De Bruyn A, Lilien G, Rangaswamy A, van Bruggen G (2009) How incorporating feedback mechanisms in a DSS affects DSS evaluations. ISR 20(4):527–546

Kayed A, El-Qawasmeh E, Qawaqneh Z (2010) Ranking web sites using domain ontology concepts. I&M 47(7–8):350–355

Kayworth T, Leidner D (2002) Leadership effectiveness in global virtual teams. JMIS 18(3):7–40

Ke W, Wei K (2008) Organizational culture and leadership in ERP implementation. DSS 45(2):208–218

Keen P (1980) MIS research: reference disciplines and a cumulative tradition. In: Proceedings of the first international conference on information systems, pp 9–18. Philadelphia

Keil M, Tan B, Wei K, Saarinen T, Tuunainen V, Wassenaar A (2000) A cross-cultural study on escalation of commitment behavior in software projects. MISQ 24(2):299–325

Keil M, Tiwana A, Bush A (2002) Reconciling user and project manager perceptions of IT project risk: a Delphi study1. ISJ 12(2):103–119

Kendall J, Kendall K (1993) Metaphors and methodologies: living beyond the systems machine. MISQ 17(2):149–171

Kerlinger F, Lee H (2000) Foundations of behavioral research. Harcourt College Publishers, Fort Worth

Kerr D, Murthy U (2009) The effectiveness of synchronous computer-mediated communication for solving hidden-profile problems: Further empirical evidence. I&M 46(2):83–89

Khazanchi D, Sutton S (2001) Assurance services for business-to- business electronic commerce: a framework and implications. JAIS 1:11

Kiang M, Kulkarni U, Tam K (1995) Self-organizing map network as an interactive clustering tool: an application to group technology. DSS 15(4):351–374

Kim D, Ferrin D, Rao R (2009) Trust and satisfaction, two stepping stones for successful e-commerce relationships: a longitudinal exploration. ISR 20(2):237–257

Kim G, Shin B, Lee H (2009) Understanding dynamics between initial trust and usage intentions of mobile banking. ISJ 19(3):283–311

Kim H, Cho J (2010) Supply chain formation using agent negotiation. DSS 49(1):77–90

Kim W (2005) On U.S. homeland security and database technology. JDM 16(1):1–17

King J, Lyytinen K (2004) Reach and grasp. MISQ 28(4):539–551

Kirsch L (1997) Portfolios of control modes and is project management. ISR 8(3):215–239

Kirsch L (2004) Deploying common systems globally: the dynamics of control. ISR 15(4):374–395

Kivijärvi H, Saarinen T (1995) Investment in information systems and the financial performance of the firm. I&M 28(2):143–163

Kivijarvi H, Zmud R (1993) DSS implementation activities, problem domain characteristics and DSS success. EJIS 2(3):159–168

Klein B, Goodhue D, Davis G (1997) Can humans detect errors in data? Impact of base rates, incentives, and goals. MISQ 21(2):169–194

Klein H, Myers M (1999) A set of principles for conducting and evaluating interpretive field studies in information systems. MISQ 23(1):67–94

Klein H, Rowe F (2008) Marshaling the professional experience of doctoral students: a contribution to the practical relevance debate. MISQ 32(4)675–686

Ko M, Osei-Bryson K (2004) Using regression splines to assess the impact of information technology investments on productivity in the health care industry. ISJ 14(1):43–63

Kocas C (2003) Evolution of prices in electronic markets under diffusion of price-comparison shopping. JMIS 19(3):99–119

Kock N, Lynn G, Dow K, Akgün A (2006) Team adaptation to electronic communication media: evidence of compensatory adaptation in new product development teams. EJIS 15(3):331–341

Koh C, Prybutok V, Zhang X (2008) Measuring e-government readiness. I&M 45(8):540–546

Koh J, Kim Y (2003) Sense of virtual community: a conceptual framework and empirical validation. IJEC 8(2):75–93

Konana P, Gupta A, Whinston A (2000) Integrating user preferences and real-time workload in information services. ISR 11(2):177–196

Kraemer K, Danziger J, King J (1993) The usefulness of computer-based information to public managers. MISQ 17(2):129–148

Kuan H, Bock G (2007) Trust transference in brick and click retailers: An investigation of the before-online-visit phase. I&M 44(2):175–187

Kuhn T (1996) The structure of scientific revolutions, 3rd edn. The University of Chicago Press, Chicago

Kulkarni U, Ravindran S, Freeze R (2007) A knowledge management success model: theoretical development and empirical validation. JMIS 23(3):309–347

Kumar A, Wainer J (2005) Meta workflows as a control and coordination mechanism for exception handling in workflow systems. DSS 40(1):89–105

Kwok R, Ma J, Vogel D (2003) Effects of group support systems and content facilitation on knowledge acquisition. JMIS 19(3):185–229

Lai H (2000) An object-oriented architecture for intelligent virtual receptionists. IJEC 4(3):69

Lamb R, Kling R (2003) Reconceptualizing users as social actors in information systems research. MISQ 27(2):197–235

Lee C, Cheng H, Cheng H (2007) An empirical study of mobile commerce in insurance industry: task–technology fit and individual differences. DSS 43(1):95–110

Lee H, Clark T, Tam K (1999a) Research report. Can EDI benefit adopters? ISR 10(2):186–195

Lee H, Lee C, Yoo C (1999b) A scenario-based object-oriented hypermedia design methodology. I&M 36(3):121–138

Lee H, Westland J, Hong S (1999c) The impact of electronic marketplaces on product prices: an empirical study of AUCNET. IJEC 4(2):45

Lee J, Kim Y (1999) Effect of partnership quality on IS outsourcing success: conceptual framework and empirical validation. JMIS 15(4):29–61

Lee J, Pi S, Kwok R, Huynh M (2003) The contribution of commitment value in internet commerce: an empirical investigation. JAIS 4:39–62

Lee S, Lim G (2005) The impact of partnership attributes on EDI implementation success. I&M 42(4):503–516

Lee S, Kim Y, Lee J (1995) An empirical study of the relationships among end-user information systems acceptance, training, and effectiveness. JMIS 12(2):189–202

Lee S, Lee K, Kang I (2005) Efficiency analysis of controls in EDI applications. I&M 42(3):425–439

Lee Y (2004) Crafting rules: context-reflective data quality problem solving. JMIS 20(3):93–119

Lee Z, Wagner C, Shin H (2008) The effect of decision support system expertise on system use behavior and performance. I&M 45(6):349–358

Legner C, Schemm J (2008) Toward the inter-organizational product information supply chain: evidence from the retail and consumer goods industries. JAIS 9(4):119–150

Leidner D, Elam J (1994) Executive information systems: their impact on executive decision making. JMIS 10(3):139–155

Leidner D, Kayworth T (2006) Review: a review of culture in information systems research—toward a theory of information technology culture conflict. MISQ 30(2):357–399

Lenard M, Madey G, Alam P (1998) The design and validation of a hybrid information system for the auditor's going concern decision. JMIS 14(4):219–237
Leroy G, Chen H (2007) Introduction to the special issue on decision support in medicine. DSS 43(4):1203–1206
Leskelä R, Teich J, Wallenius H, Wallenius J (2007) Decision support for multi-unit combinatorial bundle auctions. DSS 43(2):420–434
Levermore D, Babin G, Hsu C (2010) A new design for open and scalable collaboration of independent databases in digitally connected enterprises. JAIS 11(7):367–393
Levina N, Ross J (2003) From the vendor's perspective: exploring the value proposition in information technology outsourcing. MISQ 27(3):331–364
Lewis B, Snyder C, Rainer R (1995) An empirical assessment of the information resource management construct. JMIS 12(1):199–223
Lewis B, Templeton G, Byrd T (2005) A methodology for construct development in MIS research. EJIS 14(4):388–400
Lewis B, Templeton G, Luo X (2007) A scientometric investigation into the validity of is journal quality measures. JAIS 8(12):619–633
Li H, Ma L (2008) Visualizing decision process on spheres based on the even swap concept. DSS 45(2):354–367
Li N, Bukhres O (2005) BACIIS: biological and chemical information integration system. JDM 16(3):72–85
Li T, van Heck E, Vervest P (2009) Information capability and value creation strategy: advancing revenue management through mobile ticketing technologies. EJIS 18(1):38–51
Li X, Hitt L, Zhang Z (2011) Product reviews and competition in markets for repeat purchase products. JMIS 27(4):9–41
Liang W, Huang C (2006) Agent-based demand forecast in multi-echelon supply chain. DSS 42(1):390–407
Liang Y, West D, Stowell F (1998) An approach to object identification, selection and specification in object-oriented analysis. ISJ 8(2):163–180
Lim E, Chiang R (2004) Accommodating instance heterogeneities in database integration. DSS 38(2):213–231
Lim E, Pan S, Tan C (2005) Managing user acceptance towards enterprise resource planning (ERP) systems: understanding the dissonance between user expectations and managerial policies. EJIS 14(2):135–149
Lim V, Teo T (2009) Mind your E-manners: impact of cyber incivility on employees' work attitude and behavior. I&M 46(8):419–425
Lin C, Hsieh P (2004) A fuzzy decision support system for strategic portfolio management. DSS 38(3):383–398
Lin C, Chen H, Nunamaker J Jr (2000) Verifying the proximity and size hypothesis for self-organizing maps. JMIS 16(3):57–70
Lin F, Kuo H, Lin S (2008) The enhancement of solving the distributed constraint satisfaction problem for cooperative supply chains using multi-agent systems. DSS 45(4):795–810
Lin M, Lin Z (2006) A cost-effective critical path approach for service priority selections in grid computing economy. DSS 42(3):1628–1640
Lin Y, Gray J, Jouault F (2007) DSMDiff: a differentiation tool for domain-specific models. EJIS 16(4):349–361
Lind M, Sulek J (1998) Undersizing software systems: third versus fourth generation software development. EJIS 7(4):261–268
Liou Y, Nunamaker J Jr (1993) An investigation into knowledge acquisition using a group decision support system. I&M 24(3):121–132
Liu H, Lin F, He J, Cai Y (2010) New approach for the sequential pattern mining of high-dimensional sequence databases. DSS 50(1):270–280
Liu S, Zhang J, Keil M, Chen T (2010) Comparing senior executive and project manager perceptions of IT project risk: a Chinese Delphi study. ISJ 20(4):319–355

Ljungberg J (2000) Open source movements as a model for organising. EJIS 9(4):208–216
Lowry P, Vance A, Moody G, Beckman B, Read A (2008) Explaining and predicting the impact of branding alliances and web site quality on initial consumer trust of e-commerce web sites. JMIS 24(4):199–224
Lu J, Yu C, Liu C (2003) Learning style, learning patterns, and learning performance in a WebCT-based MIS course. I&M 40(6):497–507
Lyytinen K (1999) Empirical research in information systems: on the relevance of practice in thinking of IS research. MISQ 23(1):25–28
Lyytinen K, King J (2004) Nothing at the center? Academic legitimacy in the information systems field. JAIS 5(6):220–246
Lyytinen K, Mathiassen L (1998) Attention shaping and software risk: a categorical analysis of four classical risk management approaches. ISR 9(3):233–255
Lyytinen K, Rose G (2003) The disruptive nature of information technology innovations: the case of internet computing in systems development organizations. MISQ 27(4):557–595
Mahrer H, Krimmer R (2005) Towards the enhancement of e-democracy: identifying the notion of the "middleman paradox". ISJ 15(1):27–42
Majchrzak A, Rice R, Malhotra A, King N, Ba S (2000) Technology adaptation: the case of a computer-supported inter-organizational virtual team. MISQ 24(4):569–600
Malhotra A, Gosain S, El Sawy O (2007) Leveraging standard electronic business interfaces to enable adaptive supply chain partnerships. ISR 18(3):260–279
Malhotra N, Kim S, Agarwal J (2004) Internet users' information privacy concerns (IUIPC): the construct, the scale, and a causal model. ISR 15(4):336–355
Markus M (2001) Toward a theory of knowledge reuse: types of knowledge reuse situations and factors in reuse success. JMIS 18(1):57–93
Markus M, Robey D (1989) Information technology and organizational change: causal structure in theory and research. Manag Sci 34(5):583–598
Markus M, Majchrzak A, Gasser L (2002) A design theory for systems that support emergent knowledge processes. MISQ 26(3):179–212
Maruping L, Venkatesh V, Agarwal R (2009) A control theory perspective on agile methodology use and changing user requirements. ISR 20(3):377–399
Maruping L, Zhang X, Venkatesh V (2009) Role of collective ownership and coding standards in coordinating expertise in software project teams. EJIS 18(4):355–371
Mason R (1978) Measuring information output: a communication systems approach. I&M 1(5):219–234
Mata F, Fuerst W, Barney J (1995) Information technology and sustained competitive advantage: a resource-based analysis. MISQ 19(4):487–505
Mayer A (2009) Online social networks in economics. DSS 47(3):169–184
McKeen J, Guimaraes T, Wetherbe J (1994) The relationship between user participation and user satisfaction: an investigation of four contingency factors. MISQ 18(4):427–451
McKinney V, Yoon K, Zahedi F (2002) The measurement of web-customer satisfaction: an expectation and disconfirmation approach. ISR 13(3):296–315
McKnight D, Choudhury V, Kacmar C (2002) Developing and validating trust measures for e-commerce: an integrative typology. ISR 13(3):334–359
Mejias R, Shepherd M, Vogel D, Lazaneo L (1997) Consensus and perceived satisfaction levels: a cross-cultural comparison of GSS and Non-GSS Outcomes within and between the United States and Mexico. JMIS 13(3):137–161
Melville N, Ramirez R (2008) Information technology innovation diffusion: an information requirements paradigm. ISJ 18(3):247–273
Menczer F (2003) Complementing search engines with online web mining agents. DSS 35(2):195–212
Meng C, Pakath R (2001) The iterated prisoner's dilemma: early experiences with learning classifier system-based simple agents. DSS 31(4):379–403

Mentzer J, DeWitt W, Keebler J, Min S, Nix N, Smith C, Zacharia Z (2001) Defining supply chain management. J Bus Logistics 22(2):1–25

Miranda S, Bostrom R (1994) The impact of group support systems on group conflict and conflict management. JMIS 10(3):63–95

Mirchandani D, Pakath R (1999) Four models for a decision support system. I&M 35(1):31–42

Mitra S, Bagchi A, Bandyopadhyay A (2007) Design of a data model for social network applications. JDM 18(4):51–79

Moore G, Benbasat I (1991) Development of an instrument to measure the perceptions of adopting an information technology innovation. ISR 2(3):192–222

Moore J (2000) One road to turnover: an examination of work exhaus-tion in technology professionals. MISQ 24(1):141–168

Mosse B, Whitley E (2009) Critically classifying: UK e-government website benchmarking and the recasting of the citizen as customer. ISJ 19(2):149–173

Moukas A, Zacharia G, Guttman R, Maes P (2000) Agent-mediated electronic commerce: an mit media laboratory perspective. IJEC 4(3):5

Mudambi S, Schuff D (2010) What makes a helpful online review? A study of customer reviews on Amazon com. MISQ 34(1):185–200

Mueller J, Hutter K, Fueller J, Matzler K (2011) Virtual worlds as knowledge management platform ? A practice-perspective. ISJ 21(6):479–501

Myers M, Klein H (2011) A set of principles for conducting critical research in information systems. MISQ 35(1):17–36

Mykytyn P, Green G (1992) Effects of computer experience and task complexity on attitudes of managers. I&M 23(5):263–278

Nah F, Islam Z, Tan M (2007) Empirical assessment of factors influencing success of enterprise resource planning implementations. JDM 18(4):26–50

Nakatsu R, Iacovou C (2009) A comparative study of important risk factors involved in offshore and domestic outsourcing of software development projects: a two-panel Delphi study. I&M 46(1):57–68

Nan N, Johnston E (2009) Using multi-agent simulation to explore the contribution of facilitation to GSS transition. JAIS 10(3):252–277

Newkirk H, Lederer A, Johnson A (2008) Rapid business and IT change: drivers for strategic information systems planning? EJIS 17(3):198–218

Ngai E, Gunasekaran A (2007) A review for mobile commerce research and applications. DSS 43(1):3–15

Ngai E, Hu Y, Wong Y, Chen Y, Sun X (2011) The application of data mining techniques in financial fraud detection: a classification framework and an academic review of literature. DSS 50(3):559–569

Ngwenyama O, Lee A (1997) Communication richness in electronic mail: critical social theory and the contextuality of meaning. MISQ 21(2):145–167

Niederman F, Beise C, Beranek P (1996) Issues and concerns about computer-supported meetings: the facilitator's perspective. MISQ 20(1):1–22

Nord J, Nord G (1995) MIS research: journal status assessment and analysis. I&M 29(1):29–42

Nunamaker J Jr, Derrick D, Elkins A, Burgoon J, Patton M (2011) Embodied conversational agent–based kiosk for automated interviewing. JMIS 28(1):17–48

Oh W, Lucas H (2006) Information technology and pricing decisions: price adjustments in online computer markets. MISQ 30(3):755–775

O'Leary D (1997) Inference engine greediness: subsumption and suboptimality. DSS 21(4):263–269

Oliver J (1997) Artificial agents learn policies for multi-issue negotiation. Int J Electron Commer 1(4):49–88

Onur I, Tomak K (2006) Impact of ending rules in online auctions: the case of yahoo.com. DSS 42(3):1835–1842

Ordonez C, García-García J (2008) Referential integrity quality metrics. DSS 44(2):495–508

Orlikowski W (1992) The Duality of technology: rethinking the role of technology in organizations. Organ Sci 3(3):398–427

Orlikowski W, Baroudi J (1991) Studying information technology in organizations: research approaches and assumptions. ISR 2(1):1–28

Orlikowski W, Robey D (1991) Information technology and the structuring of organizations. ISR 2(2):143–169

Osei-Bryson K, Dong L, Ngwenyama O (2008) Exploring managerial factors affecting ERP implementation: an investigation of the Klein-Sorra model using regression splines. ISJ 18(5):499–527

Otim S, Grover V (2006) An empirical study on web-based services and customer loyalty. EJIS 15(6):527–541

Ou C, Hung S, Yen D, Liu F (2009) Impact of ATM intensity on cost efficiency: an empirical evaluation in Taiwan. I&M 46(8):442–447

Palmer J (2002) Web site usability, design, and performance metrics. ISR 13(2):151–167

Panko R, Halverson R (2001) An experiment in collaborative spreadsheet development. JAIS 2:4

Parameswaran M, Whinston A (2007) Research issues in social computing. JAIS 8(6):336–350

Parsons J (2011) An experimental study of the effects of representing property precedence on the comprehension of conceptual schemas*. JAIS 12(6):441–462

Paul D, McDaniel R (2004) A field study of the effect of interpersonal trust on virtual collaborative relationship performance. MISQ 28(2):183–227

Pauleen D (2004) An Inductively derived model of leader-initiated relationship building with virtual team members. JMIS 20(3):227–256

Pavlou P, Gefen D (2004) Building effective online marketplaces with institution-based trust. ISR 15(1):37–59

Pavri F, Ang J (1995) A study of the strategic planning practices in Singapore. I&M 28(1):33–47

Payne C (2002) On the security of open source software. ISJ 12(1):61–78

Peace A, Galletta D, Thong J (2003) Software piracy in the workplace: a model and empirical test. JMIS 20(1):153–177

Pearson J, Shim J (1994) An empirical investigation into decision support systems capabilities: a proposed taxonomy. I&M 27(1):45–57

Pendharkar P (2007) The theory and experiments of designing cooperative intelligent systems. DSS 43(3):1014–1030

Piccoli G, Ives B (2003) Trust and the unintended effects of behavior control in virtual teams. MISQ 27(3):365–395

Piccoli G, Ahmad R, Ives B (2001) Web-based virtual learning environments: a research framework and a preliminary assessment of effectiveness in basic it skills training. MISQ 25(4):401–426

Pitt L, Watson R, Kavan C (1995) Service quality: a measure of information systems effectiveness. MISQ 19(2):173–187

Polites G, Watson R (2009) Using social network analysis to analyze relationships among IS journals2. JAIS 10(8):595–636

Poon S (2000) Business environment and internet commerce benefit: a small business perspective. EJIS 9(2):72–81

Powell S, Baker K, Lawson B (2009) Impact of errors in operational spreadsheets. DSS 47(2):126–132

Prager J (2000) Linguini: language identification for multilingual documents. JMIS 16(3):71–101

Premkumar G, King W (1992) An empirical assessment of information systems planning and the role of information systems in organizations. JMIS 9(2):99–125

Premkumar G, King W (1994) The evaluation of strategic information system planning. I&M 26(6):327–340

Price R, Jensen C (2000) Extended spatiotemporal UML: motivations, requirements, and constructs. JDM 11(4):14–27

Pries-Heje J, Baskerville R (2008) The design theory nexus. MISQ 32(4):731–755

Purao S, Jain H, Nazareth D (2002) An approach to distribution of object-oriented applications in loosely coupled networks. JMIS 18(3):195–234

Purao S, Jain H, Nazareth D (2002) ODE: a tool for distributing object-oriented applications. I&M 39(8):689–703

Raghu T, Sinha R, Vinze A, Burton O (2009) Willingness to pay in an open source software environment. ISR 20(2):218–236

Rainer R, Watson H (1995) What does it take for successful executive information systems? DSS 14(2):147–156

Ramasubbu N, Mithas S, Krishnan M (2008) High tech, high touch: the effect of employee skills and customer heterogeneity on customer satisfaction with enterprise system support services. DSS 44(2):509–523

Ranganathan C, Ganapathy S (2002) Key dimensions of business-to-consumer web sites. I&M 39(6):457–465

Rao H, Pegels C, Salam A, Hwang K, Seth V (1995) The impact of EDI implementation commitment and implementation success on competitive advantage and firm performance. ISJ 5(3):185–202

Reich B, Benbasat I (2000) Factors that influence the social dimension of alignment between business and information technology objectives. MISQ 24(1):81–113

Reich B, Kaarst-Brown M (1999) Seeding the line: understanding the transition from IT to Non-IT Careers. MISQ 23(3):337–364

Ribeiro R, Moreira A, van den Broek P, Pimentel A (2011) Hybrid assessment method for software engineering decisions. DSS 51(1):208–219

Robey D (2003) Identity, legitimacy, and the dominant research paradigm: an alternative prescription for the IS discipline: a response to Benbasat and Zmud's call for returning to the IT artifact. JAIS 4(7):352–359

Rogers E (1995) Diffusion of innovations. The Free Press, New York

Röhm A, Pernul G (2000) COPS: a model and infrastructure for secure and fair electronic markets. DSS 29(4):343–355

Rosemann M, Vessey I (2008) Toward improving the relevance of information systems research to practice: the role of applicability checks. MISQ 32(1):1–22

Rustagi S, King W, Kirsch L (2008) Predictors of formal control usage in IT outsourcing partnerships. ISR 19(2):126–143

Rutner P, Hardgrave B, McKnight D (2008) Emotional dissonance and the information technology professional. MISQ 32(3):635–652

Saar-Tsechansky M, Provost F (2007) Decision-centric active learning of binary-outcome models. ISR 18(1):4–22

Sack W (2001) Conversation map: an interface for very large-scale conversations. JMIS 17(3):73–92

Santhanam R, Hartono E (2003) Issues in linking information technology capability to firm performance. MISQ 27(1):125–165

Santhanam R, Sasidharan S, Webster J (2008) Using self-regulatory learning to enhance e-learning-based information technology training. ISR 19(1):26–47

Sarker S, Lee A (2003) Using a case study to test the role of three key social enablers in ERP implementation. I&M 40(8):813–829

Scheffel T, Pikovsky A, Bichler M, Guler K (2011) An experimental comparison of linear and nonlinear price combinatorial auctions. ISR 22(2):346–368

Schmidt R, Lyytinen K, Keil M, Cule P (2001) Identifying software project risks: an international Delphi study. JMIS 17(4):5–36

Schultze U, Orlikowski W (2004) A practice perspective on technology-mediated network relations: the use of internet-based self-serve technologies. ISR 15(1):87–106

Schwaig K, Kane G, Storey V (2006) Compliance to the fair information practices: How are the Fortune 500 handling online privacy disclosures? I&M 43(7):805–820

Schweitzer L, Duxbury L (2010) Conceptualizing and measuring the virtuality of teams. ISJ 20(3):267–295

Sein M, Santhanam R (1999) Research report. Learning from goal-directed error recovery strategy. ISR 10(3):276–286

Seng J, Yao S, Hevner A (2005) Requirements-driven database systems benchmark method. DSS 38(4):629–648

Sengupta A, Venkataraman R (2011) DocBase: design, implementation and evaluation of a document database for XML. JDM 22(4):30–56

Sengupta K, Zhao J (1998) Improving the communicational effectiveness of virtual organizations through workflow automation. IJEC 3(1):49

Sexton R, Dorsey R, Sikander N (2004) Simultaneous optimization of neural network function and architecture algorithm. DSS 36(3):283–296

Shaft T, Vessey I (2006) The role of cognitive fit in the relationship between software comprehension and modification. MISQ 30(1):29–55

Shaft T, Jordan-Albert L, Jasperson J (2008) Managing change in an information systems development organization: understanding developer transitions from a structured to an object-oriented development environment. ISJ 18(3):275–297

Shanks G, Tansley E, Nuredini J, Tobin D, Weber R (2008) Representing part-whole relations in conceptual modeling: an empirical evaluation. MISQ 32(3):553–573

Shannon C, Weaver W (1949) The mathematical theory of communication. University of Illinois Press, Urbana

Sharda R, Romano N Jr, Lucca J, Weiser M, Scheets G, Chung J, Sleezer C (2004) Foundation for the study of computer-supported collaborative learning requiring immersive presence. JMIS 20(4):31–63

Sher P, Lee V (2004) Information technology as a facilitator for enhancing dynamic capabilities through knowledge management. I&M 41(8):933–945

Sherif K, Hoffman J, Thomas B (2006) Can technology build organizational social capital? The case of a global IT consulting firm. I&M 43(7):795–804

Shin K, Han I (2001) A case-based approach using inductive indexing for corporate bond rating. DSS 32(1):41–52

Shin M (2004) A framework for evaluating economics of knowledge management systems. I&M 42(1):179–196

Shin M, Huh S, Park D, Lee W (2008) Relaxing queries with hierarchical quantified data abstraction. JDM 19(4):47–61

Shrednick H, Stutt R, Weiss M (1992) Empowerment: key to IS world-class quality. MISQ 16(4):491–505

Sidorova A, Evangelopoulos N, Valacich J, Ramakrishnan T (2008) Uncovering the intellectual core of the information systems discipline. MISQ 32(3):467–482; A1–A20

Singh S, Watson H, Watson R (2002) EIS support for the strategic management process. DSS 33(1):71–85

Sinha A, May J (2005) Evaluating and timing predictive data mining models using receiver operating characteristic curves. JMIS 21(3):249–280

Sinha A, Zhao H (2008) Incorporating domain knowledge into data mining classifiers: an application in indirect lending. DSS 46(1):287–299

Siponen M, Iivari J (2006) Six design theories for IS security policies and guidelines. JAIS 7(7):445–472

Smith H, Milberg S, Burke S (1996) Information privacy: measuring individuals' concerns about organizational practices. MISQ 20(2):167–196

Smith M, Mitra S, Narasimhan S (1998) Information systems outsourcing: a study of pre-event firm characteristics. JMIS 15(2):60–93

Soffer P, Hadar I (2007) Applying ontology-based rules to conceptual modeling: a reflection on modeling decision making. EJIS 16(5):599–611

Soh C, Markus M, Goh K (2006) Electronic marketplaces and price transparency: strategy, information technology, and success. MISQ 30(3):705–723

Son J, Kim S, Riggins F (2006) Consumer adoption of net-enabled infomediaries: theoretical explanations and an empirical test. JAIS 7(7):473–508

Spears J, Barki H (2010) User participation in information systems security risk management. MISQ 34(3):503–A5

Speier C, Morris M (2003) The influence of query interface design on decision-making performance. MISQ 27(3):397–423

Staehr L (2010) Understanding the role of managerial agency in achieving business benefits from ERP systems. ISJ 20(3):213–238

Stefanou C (2001) A framework for the ex-ante evaluation of ERP software. EJIS 10(4):204–215

Storey V, Burton-Jones A, Sugumaran V, Purao S (2008) CONQUER: a methodology for context-aware query processing on the world wide web. ISR 19(1):3–25

Straub D (1989) Validating instruments in MIS research. MISQ 13(2):147–169

Straub D (1994) The Effect of culture on IT diffusion: e-mail and FAX in Japan and the U.S. ISR 5(1):23–47

Straub D, Ang S (2008) Readability and the relevance versus rigor debate. MISQ 32(4):iii–xiii

Straub D, Burton-Jones A (2007) Veni, vidi, vici: breaking the TAM logjam. JAIS 8(4):224–229

Straub D, Watson R (2001) Research commentary: transformational issues in researching IS and net-enabled organizations. ISR 12(4):337–345

Subramaniam C, Sen R, Nelson M (2009) Determinants of open source software project success: a longitudinal study. DSS 46(2):576–585

Suh K, Jenkins A (1992) A comparison of linear keyword and restricted natural language data base interfaces for novice users. ISR 3(3):252–272

Suh K, Lee Y (2005) The effects of virtual reality on consumer learning: an empirical investigation. MISQ 29(4):673–697

Suh K, Kim H, Eung K (2011) What if your avatar looks like you? Dual-congruity perspectives for avatar use. MISQ 35(3):711–A4

Susarla A, Subramanyam R, Karhade P (2010) Contractual provisions to mitigate holdup: evidence from information technology outsourcing. ISR 21(1):37–55

Tam K (1996) Dynamic price elasticity and the diffusion of mainframe computing. JMIS 13(2):163–183

Tam K, Ho S (2005) Web personalization as a persuasion strategy: an elaboration likelihood model perspective. ISR 16(3):271–291

Tan B, Watson R, Wei K (1995) National culture and group support systems: filtering communication to dampen power differentials. EJIS 4(2):82–92

Tan C, Sia S (2006) Managing flexibility in outsourcing. JAIS 7(4):179–205

Tan W, Wang K, Wong L (1998) A graphical interface to genome multi databases. JDM 9(1):24–32

Tanriverdi H (2005) Information technology relatedness knowledge management capability, and performance of multibusiness firms. MISQ 29(2):311–334

Taylor H, Dillon S, van Wingen M (2010) Focus and diversity in information systems research: meeting the dual demands of a healthy applied discipline. MISQ 34(4):647–667

Taylor S, Todd P (1995) Understanding information technology usage: a test of competing models. ISR 6(2):144–176

Teo T, King W (1997) Integration between business planning and information systems planning: an evolutionary-contingency perspective. JMIS 14(1):185–214

Teo T, Men B (2008) Knowledge portals in Chinese consulting firms: a task-technology fit perspective. EJIS 17(6):557–574

Thatcher M, Oliver J (2001) The impact of technology investments on a firm's production efficiency, product quality, and productivity. JMIS 18(2):17–45

Tomiuk D, Pinsonneault A (2009) Applying relationship theories to web site design: development and validation of a site-communality scale. ISJ 19(4):413–435

Torkzadeh G, Doll W (1993) The place and value of documentation in end-user computing. I&M 24(3):147–158
Towell E, Haseman W (1995) Implementation of an interface to multiple databases. JDM 6(2):13–21
Trice A, Davis R (1993) Heuristics for reconciling independent knowledge bases. ISR 4(3):262–288
Tsai J, Egelman S, Cranor L, Acquisti A (2011) The effect of online privacy information on purchasing behavior: an experimental study. ISR 22(2):254–268
Tung L, Quaddus M (2002) Cultural differences explaining the differences in results in GSS: implications for the next decade. DSS 33(2):177–199
Tung Y, Gopal R, Marsden J (1999) HypEs: an architecture for hypermedia-enabled expert systems. DSS 26(4):307–321
Tuunainen V (1998) Opportunities of effective integration of EDI for small businesses in the automotive industry. I&M 34(6):361–375
Udo G, Guimaraes T (1994) Empirically assessing factors related to DSS benefits. EJIS 3(3):218–227
Usunier J, Roulin N, Ivens B (2009) Cultural, national, and industry-level differences in B2B web site design and content. IJEC 14(2):41–87
Van der Aalst W, Kumar A (2003) XML-based schema definition for support of interorganizational workflow. ISR 14(1):23–46
van Dyke T, Kappelman L, Prybutok V (1997) Measuring information systems service quality: concerns on the use of the SERVQUAL questionnaire. MISQ 21(2):195–208
Van Slyke C, Ilie V, Lou H, Stafford T (2007) Perceived critical mass and the adoption of a communication technology. EJIS 16(3):270–283
Vance A (2012) The end of free will. Bloomberg Businessweek. 16 Sept 2012, pp 86–87.
Varshney U (2008) A middleware framework for managing transactions in group-oriented mobile commerce services. DSS 46(1):356–365
Venkatesh V (2000) Determinants of perceived ease of use: integrating control, intrinsic motivation, and emotion into the technology acceptance model. ISR 11(4):342–365
Venkatesh V, Davis F (2000) A theoretical extension of the technology acceptance model: four longitudinal field studies. Manage Sci 46(2):186–204
Venkatesh V, Morris M, Davis G, Davis F (2003) User acceptance of information technology: toward a unified view. MISQ 27(3):425–478
Vessey I, Ramesh V, Glass R (2002) Research in information systems: an empirical study of diversity in the discipline and its journals. JMIS 19(2):129–174
Von Hippel E (1994) Sticky information and the locus of problem solving: implications for innovation. Manage Sci 40(4):429–439
von Solms R, van der Haar H, von Solms S, Caelli W (1994) A framework for information security evaluation. I&M 26(3):143–153
Wade M, Biehl M, Kim H (2006) Information systems is ^not a reference discipline (and what we can do about it). JAIS 7(5):247–268
Wagner C, Majchrzak A (2007) Enabling customer-centricity using wikis and the wiki way. JMIS 23(3):17–43
Wakefield R, Leidner D, Garrison G (2008) Research note: a model of conflict, leadership, and performance in virtual teams. ISR 19(4):434–455
Walczak S (2001) An empirical analysis of data requirements for financial forecasting with neural networks. JMIS 17(4):203–222
Wallace L, Keil M, Rai A (2004) Understanding software project risk: a cluster analysis. I&M 42(1):115–125
Wang C, Ahmed P, Rafiq M (2008) Knowledge management orientation: construct development and empirical validation. EJIS 17(3):219–235
Wang E, Klein G, Jiang J (2006) ERP misfit: country of origin and organizational factors. JMIS 23(1):263–292

Wang J, Chaudhury A, Rao H (2008) A value-at-risk approach to information security investment. ISR 19(1):106–120
Wang M, Vogel D, Ran W (2011) Creating a performance-oriented e-learning environment: a design science approach. I&M 48(7):260–269
Wang S (1996) Toward formalized object-oriented management information systems analysis. JMIS 12(4):117–141
Wang W, Benbasat I (2005) Trust in and adoption of online recommendation agents. JAIS 6(3):72–101
Wang Y, Lin H, Luarn P (2006) Predicting consumer intention to use mobile service. ISJ 16(2):157–179
Warkentin M, Beranek P (1999) Training to improve virtual team communication. ISJ 9(4):271–289
Watson R, Kelly G, Galliers R, Brancheau J (1997) Key issues in information systems management: an international perspective. JMIS 13(4):91–117
Watson-Manheim M, Belanger F (2007) Communication media repertoires: dealing with the multiplicity of media choices. MISQ 31(2):267–293
Webster J, Martocchio J (1992) Microcomputer playfulness: development of a measure with workplace implications. MISQ 16(2):201–226
Wei C, Yang C, Lin C (2008) A latent semantic indexing-based approach to multilingual document clustering. DSS 45(3):606–620
Wei H, Wang E (2010) The strategic value of supply chain visibility: increasing the ability to reconfigure. EJIS 19(2):238–256
Weill P (1992) The relationship between investment in information technology and firm performance: a study of the valve manufacturing sector. ISR 3(4):307–333
Weippl E, Klug L, Essmayr W (2003) A new approach to secure federated information bases using agent technology. JDM 14(1):48–68
Wernerfelt B (1984) A resource-based view of the firm. Strateg Manag J 5(2):171–180
West D (1992) Knowledge elicitation as an inquiring system: towards a 'subjective' knowledge elicitation methodology. ISJ 2(1):31–44
West L Jr (1997) Electronic markets and electronic governments. IJEC 2(2):5
Westland J (1992) Self-organizing executive information networks. DSS 8(1):41–53
Westland J (2004) The cost behavior of software defects. DSS 37(2):229–238
Wilde W, Swatman P (1997) Toward virtual communities in rural Australia. IJEC 2(1):43
Willcocks L, Kern T (1998) IT outsourcing as strategic partnering: the case of the United Kingdom inland revenue. EJIS 7(1):29–45
Wilson R, Sharda R (1994) Bankruptcy prediction using neural networks. DSS 11(5):545–557
Winter S, Chudoba K, Gutek B (1997) Misplaced resources? Factors associated with computer literacy among end-users. I&M 32(1):29–42
Wixom B, Todd P (2005) A theoretical integration of user satisfaction and technology acceptance. ISR 16(1):85–102
Wu C, Chan H, Teo H, Wei K (1994) An experimental study of object-oriented query language and relational query language for novice users. JDM 5(4):16–27
Wu I, Li J, Fu C (2011) The adoption of mobile healthcare by hospital's professionals: an integrative perspective. DSS 51(3):587–596
Wu J, Shin S, Heng M (2007) A methodology for ERP misfit analysis. I&M 44(8):666–680
Xiao B, Benbasat I (2007) E-commerce product recommendation agents: use, characteristics, and impact. MISQ 31(1):137–209
Xiao B, Benbasat I (2011) Product-related deception in e-commerce: a theoretical perspective. MISQ 35(1):169–196
Xu H, Teo H, Tan B, Agarwal R (2010) The role of push–pull technology in privacy calculus: the case of location-based services. JMIS 26(3):135–173
Xu P, Ramesh B (2007) Software process tailoring: an empirical investigation. JMIS 24(2):293–328

Yang Z, Cai S, Zhou Z, Zhou N (2005) Development and validation of an instrument to measure user perceived service quality of information presenting web portals. I&M 42(4):575–589
Yau C, Davis T (1994) Using multi-criteria analysis for tenant selection. DSS 12(3):233–244
Ye L, Johnson P (1995) The impact of explanation facilities on user acceptance of expert systems advice. MISQ 19(2):157–172
Yen B (2007) The design and evaluation of accessibility on web navigation. DSS 42(4):2219–2235
Yoo B, Choudhary V, Mukhopadhyay T (2003) A Model of neutral B2B intermediaries. JMIS 19(3):43–68
Yoo Y, Alavi M (2001) Media and group cohesion: relative influences on social pretense, task participation, and group consensus. MISQ 25(3):371–390
Yoon Y, Guimaraes T, O'Neal Q (1995) Exploring the factors associated with expert systems success. MISQ 19(1):83–106
Yu L, Lai K (2011) A distance-based group decision-making methodology for multi-person multi-criteria emergency decision support. DSS 51(2):307–315
Yuan Y, Archer N, Connelly C, Zheng W (2010) Identifying the ideal fit between mobile work and mobile work support. I&M 47(3):125–137
Zahedi F, Bansal G (2011) Cultural signifiers of web site images. JMIS 28(1):147–200
Zhang H, Kishore R, Ram R (2007) Semantics of the MibML conceptual modeling grammar: an ontological analysis using the Bunge-Wang-Weber framework. JDM 18(1):1–19
Zhang J, Bandyopadhyay S, Piramuthu S (2008) Real option valuation on grid computing. DSS 46(1):333–343
Zhou Y, Qin J, Chen H (2006) CMedPort: an integrated approach to facilitating Chinese medical information seeking. DSS 42(3):1431–1448
Zhu K (2004) The complementarity of information technology infrastructure and e-commerce capability: a resource-based assessment of their business value. JMIS 21(1):167–202
Zhu K, Kraemer K (2002) E-commerce metrics for net-enhanced organizations: assessing the value of e-commerce to firm performance in the manufacturing sector. ISR 13(3):275–295
Zhu K, Dong S, Xu S, Kraemer K (2006) Innovation diffusion in global contexts: determinants of post-adoption digital transformation of European companies. EJIS 15(6):601–616
Zhuang Y, Lederer A (2003) An instrument for measuring the business benefits of e-commerce retailing. IJEC 7(3):65–99
Zigurs I, Buckland B (1998) A theory of task/technology fit and group support systems effectiveness. MISQ 22(3):313–334
Zwass V (1996) Electronic commerce: structures and issues. IJEC 1(1):3–23

MIX
Papier aus verantwortungsvollen Quellen
Paper from responsible sources
FSC® C105338

If you have any concerns about our products,
you can contact us on
ProductSafety@springernature.com

In case Publisher is established outside the EU,
the EU authorized representative is:
Springer Nature Customer Service Center GmbH
Europaplatz 3, 69115 Heidelberg, Germany

Printed by Libri Plureos GmbH
in Hamburg, Germany